W9-AWM-006

THE FRENCH MARKET

THE FRENCH MARKET

More Recipes from a French Kitchen

Joanne Harris and Fran Warde

WILLIAM MORROW

An Imprint of HarperCollins*Publishers*

Originally published in 2005 by Transworld Publishers, a division of
The Random House Group Ltd.

THE FRENCH MARKET. Copyright © 2005, 2006 by Joanne Harris and Fran Warde.

All rights reserved. Printed in Singapore. No part of this book may be used or reproduced
in any manner whatsoever without written permission except in the case of brief quotations
embodied in critical articles and reviews. For information address HarperCollins Publishers,
10 East 53rd Street, New York, NY 10022.

HarperCollins books may be purchased for educational, business, or sales promotional use.
For information please write: Special Markets Department, HarperCollins Publishers,
10 East 53rd Street, New York, NY 10022.

FIRST U.S. EDITION PUBLISHED 2006

Printed on acid-free paper

Library of Congress Cataloging-in-Publication Data
Harris, Joanne, 1964–
   The French market : more recipes from a French kitchen /
Joanne Harris and Fran Warde.—1st U.S. ed.
      p.   cm.
   Includes index.
   ISBN-13: 978-0-06-089313-2
   ISBN-10: 0-06-089313-3
   1. Cookery, French.   I. Warde, Fran.   II. Title.

TX719.H268 2005
641.5944—dc22   2005057500

06 07 08 09 10 WBC/IM 10 9 8 7 6 5 4 3 2 1

Contents

Introduction

Surely one of the joys of visiting any country must be the discovery of that country's food. It's the simplest and most effective way to embrace a culture; languages and customs take time to learn, but the gift of food is both immediate and very personal, and the acceptance (or rejection) of that gift may sometimes determine an entire future relationship with the country, its people, and its traditions.

My great-grandmother had a particularly simple way of judging character. Supremely unmoved by such things as status, beauty, wealth, or influence, she would base her first impression of any guest on one thing—how they behaved at table. If they ate well, they were invited a second time. If not, we never saw them again. Her motto was *Who eats well, lives well,* and it's astonishing how often her judgment proved correct.

My great-grandmother's recipes were such favorites with our family that I included a number of them in *My French Kitchen*—so many, in fact, that when Fran and I began to plan our second cookbook, we realized that I had run out of recipes from my own family. Fortunately, every family, like every region, has its particular traditions, and for this new project Fran and I decided to head for the southwest of France and to take what inspiration we

could from families, communities, and markets there.

It's a region I have come to know very well. My grandfather had friends in Nérac, on the river Baïse, and from my first visit I was enchanted by the little town with its crooked half-timbered buildings, its old tanneries and cobbled squares, and the multitude of little flat-bottomed boats that drifted downriver. I welcomed this opportunity to discover it further, and the recipes in this book come to us from the winemakers, farmers, and many other locals who threw themselves so wholeheartedly into this project with us.

There is a saying here that goes "Fishermen and Gascons are born to lie." That seems appropriate to Nérac, where *gasconnades* abound (the exuberantly tall tales in which the region specializes), and, if you believe what you hear, every fisherman is descended from a king (or at least a prince) in exile.

There is some reason to believe it; Henri IV lived in Nérac as a young man, and the tales of his many seductions are widespread around the region. Catherine de Médici and Marguerite de Valois were frequent visitors. Even Shakespeare stayed here for a time and is said to have written *Love's Labour Lost* in the Garenne, Henri IV's royal park. Alexandre Dumas, creator of d'Artagnan, the most

famous Gascon of all, lived close by and passionate gourmet that he was, wrote his *Grand Dictionnaire de Cuisine* just a few miles away. As a fellow author of both novels and cookbooks I feel a particular kinship with Dumas—now there was a man who really enjoyed the various pleasures life had to offer. His writing reflects this, and the inhabitants of the region are proud to claim him as one of their adopted sons.

It's certainly true that this little stretch of the river Baïse is a place where recipes, stories, myths, and lies are equally celebrated. The river brings them, like flotsam, and the fertile soil helps them grow. One of these stories became a book called *Chocolat*, which in turn began a chain of other stories, which in turn led Fran and I back here.

Today, I am delighted to see how little has altered. Cafés, shops, streets—even the *chocolaterie* La Cigale, where Monsieur and Madame Sarrauste have made their own chocolates for more than thirty years—all seem quite unchanged. There is some tourism, but not an excessive amount; even the riverboats are still as I remember them, with their groups of colorful—and sometimes unwelcome— travelers. Most of all I remember the markets. Along the Baïse there is a market every day: flower markets, fruit and vegetable markets, and special markets

dedicated to geese, ducks, foie gras, Armagnac, or honey. Children are especially welcome; as a small child I frequently spent my mornings at one market or another sampling the various delicacies. If I had wanted, I could easily have lived for an entire holiday on nothing more than these gifts of fruit, bread, cake, and cheese so generously handed out to *la petite Anglaise.* Of course, to any seller, the pulling power of a small girl by their market stall, enthusiastically eating melon, cake, peaches, or plums, had to be worth any number of free samples.

It is from the markets of this region that Fran and I have taken our main inspiration for this cookbook. The market lies at the heart of any rural community. It is a meeting place, an exchange of gossip, an excuse for celebration, for music, for wine tasting, and for the telling of stories. Here contacts are made, recipes exchanged, extravagant flirtations conducted. Our plan was to scour the markets of the Baïse and its neighboring regions and to collect ideas, recipes, specialties—and, of course, stories—wherever we went.

It wasn't difficult. The markets of France are a chef's dream: an intoxicating display of seasonal produce, dazzling colors, savory scents. Everyone is in

competition: the cheese vendor, selling air-dried goat cheese flavored with fennel. The sellers of dried meats: saucisson with black currants, garlic, or mushrooms; strings of peppery salami. Everything is so tempting; the stalls selling brioche, honey, and the little sweets called *Amours de Fleurette* (there's a story there, too, of a local girl seduced by a young prince, whose tragic death is still commemorated in sugar and chocolate). Here fruit and vegetables still depend on the seasons; a festival celebrates the first cherries, the new asparagus, the autumn mushrooms. In England, it's all too easy to forget the seasons—lured by the promise of out-of-season strawberries or watery tomatoes or floury-tasting apples with little to recommend them but regularity of shape.

Here the wares are anything but regular. Huge, misshapen Marmande tomatoes; giant purple eggplants; striped melons; fat golden-skinned kiwis; raspberries so ripe that they almost disintegrate to the touch. Most farmers use the traditional methods; many openly flout regulations by selling nonstandard, unapproved varieties of fruit and vegetables. Cheeses are defiantly unpasteurized; geese and ducks are reared by hand; cash crops imposed two or three decades ago are gradually being replaced by truffle oaks, fruit trees, and rediscovered varieties of potatoes.

This return to tradition has caused some friction between the locals and officials of the European Union. One beekeeper, a man of seventy, told me the sad story of how the authorities had used E.U. regulations to ban him from selling the traditionally produced honey that has been his family's livelihood for three generations.

"How do you manage?" I asked him.

"Oh, I sell postcards now. Five euros each."

"Five euros? Isn't that a bit steep for just one postcard?"

"Perhaps," he said, with a gleam in his eye. "But each one comes with a free pot of honey."

It is this Gascon spirit of enjoyment, tradition, and enterprise that Fran and I have tried to capture in *The French Market*. Most of the recipes are simple; all are based on the idea that with good seasonal ingredients at hand, no chef can go far wrong; and all are designed to be tried, tested, adapted, and re-created to suit you, your kitchen, and the company you keep.

Soups and Starters

Soups are a wonderful way of using the many and varied seasonal vegetables that are one of the principal joys of the French market. Pumpkins, mushrooms, chestnuts, and squash in autumn; fava beans, sweet green peas, and watercress in summer; sweet potatoes, green beans, celery root, and carrots throughout the winter. Some of these soups are designed to form the basis of an entire meal, while others serve to stimulate the palate in readiness for the main course. In both cases, they are all delicious, simple, and extremely satisfying to make.

The better the stock, the tastier the soup, so make your own if you can. For homemade stock, take the bones or carcass from beef, chicken, or lamb (do not mix), place in a large pot, cover with water, and add onion, carrot, leek, bay leaf, thyme, salt, and pepper. Bring to a boil, then simmer for 1½ hours, strain, and let cool. Skim off any fat that floats to the surface.

The light dishes that follow the soups are ideal with crudités for quick, simple summer dishes or could be served as individual small courses as part of a more substantial celebration meal.

SOUPE PRINTANIÈRE

SPRING HARVEST SOUP WITH FAVA BEANS

This fresh, creamy green soup celebrates the arrival of spring's first fava beans, so tender they can be eaten raw.

Serves 6

2 tablespoons olive oil
3 onions, finely chopped
4 slices bacon, diced
2 garlic cloves, chopped
5 cups chicken or vegetable stock
3 pounds fresh fava beans, shelled
Sea salt, to taste
Freshly ground black pepper, to taste
A bunch of fresh flat-leaf parsley, leaves
    chopped

Heat the oil in a large pot over medium-high heat. Add the onions and bacon and cook until the onions are browned, about 5 minutes. Add the garlic and cook for 2 minutes more. Stir in the stock and about three-quarters of the beans. Bring to a boil. Reduce the heat to low, and simmer until the beans are tender, about 30 minutes. Blend in a blender until smooth and return to the pot. Add the remaining beans and simmer for 5 minutes. Season with the salt and pepper. Sprinkle with the parsley, mix well, and serve hot.

SOUPE AU CHOU-FLEUR

CAULIFLOWER SOUP

This luscious, creamy white soup is best made with the freshest, youngest cauliflower of the season. The tender slices of Brie melt into the soup to make an even more luxurious consistency.

Serves 6

2 tablespoons unsalted butter
3 celery ribs, diced
2 shallots, diced
1 large cauliflower, trimmed and cut
    into florets
5 cups chicken or vegetable stock
1 teaspoon Dijon mustard
3 sprigs of fresh thyme
2 bay leaves
¾ cup half-and-half
Sea salt, to taste
Freshly ground black pepper, to taste
Freshly grated nutmeg, to taste
4 ounces Brie, thinly sliced
Chopped fresh chives

Melt the butter in a large pot over medium heat, add the celery and shallots, and cook without browning for 5 minutes. Add the cauliflower, stock, mustard, thyme, and bay leaves and bring to a boil. Reduce the heat to low and simmer until the cauliflower is tender, about 20 minutes. Remove the thyme and bay leaves, and puree the soup in a blender. Return to the pot, stir in the half-and-half, and heat through. Season with the salt, pepper, and nutmeg. Serve hot, garnished with the Brie and chives.

SOUPE AUX MOULES

MUSSEL SOUP

This thick, rich soup of mussels, saffron, wine, and cream works especially well with chile garlic bread, which is Anouchka's favorite, or with thick slices of country bread. Personally, I prefer to serve the soup with most of the mussels in their shells; I think that one of the pleasures of eating mussels is the time that it takes and the voluptuous sensation of eating with your fingers. Try it both ways and see which you like best.

Serves 6

3 tablespoons olive oil
3 shallots, chopped
2 garlic cloves, chopped
⅓ cup all-purpose flour
2 cups fish stock
A generous pinch of saffron
⅓ cup heavy cream
¾ cup dry white wine
4 pounds mussels, scrubbed
Sea salt, to taste
Freshly ground black pepper, to taste
A bunch of flat-leaf parsley, leaves
    chopped

Heat the oil in a soup pot over medium-low heat and gently cook the shallots until softened, about 4 minutes. Add the garlic and cook for 1 minute more. Sprinkle in the flour and stir well. Slowly whisk in the stock to make a smooth, thick sauce. Whisk in the saffron and cream and simmer for 15 minutes.

Meanwhile, bring the wine to a boil in another pot over high heat. Add the mussels and cover. Cook until the mussels open, about 6 minutes. Discard any mussels that do not open.

Drain the mussels in a colander, reserving the cooking liquid. Strain the liquid through a fine wire sieve into the soup. When the mussels are cool enough to handle, remove the meat from the shells, and add to the soup. Simmer for 2 minutes. Season with the salt and pepper. Stir in the parsley and serve hot.

SOUPE AUX HARICOTS

WHITE BEAN SOUP

Fran likes to use white cannellini beans for this recipe, although white navy beans (which are similar in taste, though a little smaller) will do just as well. Choose the tastiest tomatoes you can find— we use enormous misshapen Marmande tomatoes in France, but any big, juicy beefsteak or red heirloom tomatoes will do.

10 ounces (about 1¼ cups) dried white
    kidney (cannellini) or navy beans, soaked
    overnight in a generous amount of water
5 cups chicken stock
2 onions, chopped
2 garlic cloves, chopped
¾ pound boneless dry-cured ham, such
    as prosciutto, chopped
2 tablespoons olive oil
1¾ pounds ripe tomatoes
3 sprigs of fresh thyme
2 bay leaves
Sea salt, to taste
Freshly ground black pepper, to taste
A bunch of flat-leaf parsley, leaves chopped

Drain and rinse the beans and put them in a soup pot. Add the stock, onions, garlic, ham, and olive oil and bring to a boil over high heat. Reduce the heat to low and simmer while preparing the tomatoes.

    Bring a large pot of water to a boil. In batches, add the tomatoes and boil for 20 seconds or so to loosen the skin. Remove with a slotted spoon, and peel, seed, and coarsely chop the tomatoes. Add to the beans, along with the thyme and bay leaves. Simmer until the beans are tender, about 1½ hours. Remove the thyme and bay leaves. Season with the salt and pepper. Stir in the parsley and serve hot.

POTAGE BONNE FEMME

THE GOOD WIFE'S SOUP

The good wife in this case is Madame Labadie of Nérac, who grows the biggest and best leeks in the entire region. The recipe has been slightly adapted with low-fat cream cheese, which stands in for the French fromage frais. *But to be entirely authentic, use two* Vache qui Rit *(Laughing Cow) cheese triangles instead of Neufchâtel. Madame Labadie has been making soup this way since the war, and completely disapproves of such frivolities as low-fat cheese. In an emergency, she concedes that the other cheeses could work almost as well as her favorite.*

Serves 6

2 tablespoons unsalted butter
1 pound leeks, white and pale green parts
    only, cut into matchsticks
1¼ pounds baking potatoes, peeled and
    diced
2 tablespoons all-purpose flour
1 quart chicken or vegetable stock
Sea salt, to taste
Freshly ground black pepper, to taste
2 small triangles Laughing Cow cheese or
    2 ounces low-fat cream cheese
Chopped fresh chives and flat-leaf parsley
    leaves, to serve

Melt the butter in a soup pot over medium heat. Add the leeks and potatoes and cook for a few minutes until the leeks soften without browning. Sprinkle in the flour and mix well. Slowly add the stock, stirring well, and bring to a boil. Season with the salt and pepper and reduce the heat to medium-low. Simmer gently until the potatoes are tender, about 20 minutes. If you like a smooth consistency, puree in a blender, and return to the pot. Stir in the cheese, chives, and parsley and serve hot.

SOUPE DU VIGNERON

THE WINEMAKER'S SOUP

This lovely autumn recipe is typical of southwestern France, and combines the season's first wild mushrooms with the region's favorite specialty— wine. Use white wine for a lighter, sweeter taste and red for a richer, darker flavor.

Serves 6

4 tablespoons unsalted butter
¼ cup olive oil
1½ pounds onions, thinly sliced
½ pound wild (such as chanterelle) or
    cremini mushrooms, sliced
3 garlic cloves, chopped
3 cups chicken or vegetable stock
2 cups dry red or white wine
3 sprigs of fresh thyme
2 bay leaves
Sea salt, to taste
Freshly ground black pepper, to taste
6 slices day-old crusty bread, cut into cubes

Heat the butter and oil in a soup pot over medium heat. Add the onions and cook, stirring often, until soft and golden, about 20 minutes. Add the mushrooms and garlic and cook for 10 minutes more. Stir in the stock, wine, thyme, and bay leaves. Season with salt and pepper and bring to a boil over high heat. Reduce the heat to low and simmer for 45 minutes. Remove the thyme and bay leaves. Place a slice of bread in each of six soup bowls and ladle in the soup. Serve hot.

GARBURE

This is a hearty soup recipe from the southwest of France. Everyone has a slightly different version of it, but it should always be rich, thick, tasty, and satisfying. It is one of those dishes that is best reheated, so if you can't resist eating it all right away, double the amount.

Serves 6

10 ounces (about 1¼ cups) dried white kidney (cannellini) beans
1 pound dry-cured ham, such as prosciutto, diced
2 onions, chopped
2 garlic cloves, chopped
1 bouquet garni (sprigs of fresh thyme, parsley, sage, marjoram, and a bay leaf tied into a bundle with kitchen twine)
¾ pound baking potatoes, peeled and diced
1 pound fresh fava beans in pods, shelled
¼ head medium green cabbage (about ½ pound), cored and chopped
2 tablespoons rendered duck or chicken fat or fat from canned confit
Sea salt, to taste
Freshly ground black pepper, to taste
6 slices crusty whole wheat bread, cubed
10 ounces Roquefort, crumbled

Soak the beans overnight in plenty of cold water. Drain and rinse the beans. Place them in a large saucepan with the ham, 5 cups water, onions, garlic, and bouquet garni. Cover and bring to a boil over high heat. Reduce the heat to medium-low and simmer for 1½ hours. Stir in the potatoes, fava beans, cabbage, and duck fat and simmer until the potatoes are tender, about 45 minutes more. Season the soup with salt—although sometimes the ham has enough salt in it for this to be unnecessary—and pepper. Put the bread in the soup bowls and top with the cheese. Ladle in the soup and serve hot.

GOUGÈRE AU JAMBON

The traditional gougère, made from choux pastry, is baked as a single large ring, although you could also make it as a number of little puffs. Either way, it is simple to make, and works with a simple green salad or as an apéritif with a glass of wine. For simplicity's sake, I have made this gougère in an ovenproof dish that roughly shapes the dough and makes an easy and tasty supper dish.

Serves 6

For the cream puff dough
1 cup water
8 tablespoons (1 stick) unsalted butter,
    thinly sliced
1 cup all-purpose flour
4 large eggs, beaten, at room temperature
½ cup shredded Beaufort or Gruyère
    (2 ounces)

For the ham filling
2 tablespoons olive oil
1 tablespoon unsalted butter
2 shallots, chopped
2 garlic cloves, chopped
3 tablespoons all-purpose flour
⅔ cup ham or chicken stock
⅓ cup dry white wine
2 teaspoons whole grain mustard
Freshly ground black pepper, to taste
1 pound cooked ham, roughly diced

Heat the oven to 400°F. Butter an 11- by 8½-inch shallow baking dish.

To make the cream puff dough, bring the water and butter to a boil in a medium saucepan over high heat. Remove from the heat and stir until the butter melts. Add the flour and rapidly beat until the mixture is smooth. Return to medium-low heat and beat constantly until the mixture pulls away from the pan. Remove from the heat and cool for 5 minutes. Gradually beat in the eggs until the dough drops easily from the spoon (you may not use all of the eggs). Stir in the cheese. Spoon the dough around the edge of the prepared dish. Bake until puffed and golden, about 30 minutes.

Meanwhile, make the filling. Heat the oil and butter in a skillet over medium heat. Add the shallots and cook until tender, about 3 minutes, then add the garlic and cook for 1 minute. Remove the pan from the heat, sprinkle in the flour, and mix well. Return to low heat and gradually mix in the stock, then the wine, mustard, and pepper. Bring to a full boil, stirring constantly to avoid sticking. Stir in the ham. Set aside until the pastry is ready. Spoon the filling into the center of the dish. Reduce the heat to 300°F and continue baking until the pastry is golden brown and the filling is bubbling, about 25 minutes more. Serve hot.

FEUILLETÉ AU FROMAGE

PUFF PASTRY WITH CHEESE

This dish combines the typical inland flavors of thyme, smoked bacon, and regional cheeses with a light, flaky pastry base. Don't stress too much over the puff pastry; if you don't have the time to make your own, the store-bought variety works just as well.

For the puff pastry
1¾ cups all-purpose flour
Pinch of salt
½ cup ice-cold water, as needed
1 teaspoon fresh lemon juice
1 cup plus 2 tablespoons (2¼ sticks) unsalted butter, at cool room temperature

For the filling
2 tablespoons olive oil
2 pounds red onions, thinly sliced
½ cup dry white wine
7 ounces slab bacon, rind trimmed and discarded, cut into thick strips (optional)
3 sprigs of fresh thyme
4 ounces Port Salut or Chaumes, sliced

1 large egg, beaten, for glazing the pastry
Sea salt, to taste
Freshly ground black pepper, to taste

To make the pastry, sift the flour and salt into a medium bowl and make a well in the center. Mix the water and lemon juice, and stir enough into the flour to make a smooth dough. Gather into a rectangle, wrap in plastic wrap, and refrigerate for 30 minutes. Meanwhile, knead the butter into a rough rectangle, and place it between two sheets of plastic wrap. Using a rolling pin, flatten the butter into an 8- by 6-inch rectangle, and refrigerate with the dough. On a lightly floured work surface, roll out the dough into a 10- by 18-inch rectangle. Place the butter rectangle in the center of the dough and fold the two ends in to cover the butter. Turn the dough 90 degrees, and roll out again into a 10- by 18-inch rectangle. Fold one-third up and the other third down (like a letter), turn 90 degrees, and roll out again. Wrap in plastic wrap and refrigerate for 30 minutes. Repeat the double rolling process and refrigeration period twice.

To make the filling, heat the oil in a large skillet over medium-high heat. Add the onions and cook briskly for 5 minutes. Add the wine, bacon, if using, and 2 sprigs of thyme. Reduce the heat to medium-low and cook until the liquid has evaporated, about 30 minutes. Remove the thyme sprigs.

Heat the oven to 425°F. On a lightly floured surface, roll out the pastry into an 8½- by 12-inch rectangle. Place on a baking sheet, pierce all over with a fork, then score the border with a fine-bladed dinner knife. Bake for 12 minutes. Remove and cover the top of the pastry with the onions, cheese, and the leaves of the remaining thyme sprig, leaving a 1-inch border of pastry. Lightly brush the exposed pastry with some of the egg. Season with salt and pepper. Bake for 15 minutes more. Reduce the heat to 325°F and bake until the pastry is puffed and golden brown, about 15 minutes more. Serve hot.

TARTELETTES AUX CHAMPIGNONS DES BOIS

WILD MUSHROOM TARTLETS

*There are so many different kinds of mushrooms
available at different times of year that you can
afford to be creative with this recipe, although
it's always best to choose whatever is fresh and in
season. Chanterelles have a subtle apricot scent;
cèpes a rich, almost meaty taste, and the
wonderfully named* trompettes de la mort
*have a strong, wild flavor that works very well
in this colorful autumn dish.*

Serves 6

For the tartlet shells
Puff Pastry (page 32)

For the mushroom filling
4 tablespoons unsalted butter
3 shallots, very finely chopped
1 pound assorted wild mushrooms
3 garlic cloves, chopped
¼ cup dry white wine
¼ cup heavy cream
Sea salt, to taste
Freshly ground black pepper, to taste
A bunch of flat-leaf parsley, leaves chopped

For the puff pastry tartlet shells, prepare the
puff pastry as directed. Heat the oven to 425°F.
On a lightly floured work surface, roll out the
pastry into a 12- by 16-inch rectangle. Cut into
6 equal-sized rectangles about 6 by 5½ inches
each. Prick each pastry rectangle all over with a
fork (this helps keep the pastry flat while
baking). Cut a ¾-inch strip from around the
edge of each piece. Brush the edges of each
rectangle with beaten egg, and lay the thin
strips back on the pastry base, like a picture
frame. Using a fine-bladed dinner knife, score
the edge of each pastry with horizontal marks;
this helps the pastry to rise and form a neat
edge. Place on a baking sheet. Bake until
golden, 12 to 15 minutes. Set aside at room
temperature until ready to serve.

For the filling, melt the butter in a large
skillet over medium-low heat. Add the shallots
and cook until tender without browning, about
3 minutes. Add the mushrooms and garlic and
increase the heat to medium-high. Cook until
the mushrooms begin to soften, about
5 minutes. Set aside until ready to serve.

To serve, heat the oven to 350°F. Return
the pastry shells to the oven to heat through,
about 4 minutes. Return the mushrooms to a
simmer over high heat. Add the wine and
cream, bring to a simmer, and heat for 1
minute. Season with salt and pepper and stir in
the parsley. Place each tartlet shell on a plate,
fill with the mushrooms, and serve at once.

BRIOCHE AUX CHAMPIGNONS

BRIOCHE WITH MUSHROOMS

This recipe calls for the largest and tastiest mushrooms you can find. As an alternative to the mushrooms listed here, try the incomparable fresh porcini, which by itself tastes good enough to turn the most committed carnivore into a vegetarian.

Serves 6

4 tablespoons unsalted butter
3 tablespoons olive oil
12 large stemmed shiitake mushrooms
8 ounces chanterelles
2 garlic cloves, chopped
⅓ cup dry white wine
3 tablespoons heavy cream
Sea salt, to taste
Freshly ground black pepper, to taste
6 slices brioche, toasted
Chopped chives, for garnish

Heat the butter and olive oil in a large skillet over medium heat. Add the shiitakes and cook, stirring occasionally, for 8 minutes. Add the chanterelles and cook for 3 minutes more. Add the garlic and cook for 1 minute. Add the wine and cream and season with salt and pepper. Bring to a boil over high heat. Cook until the liquid evaporates and thickens, about 2 minutes.

Place the brioche on individual plates. Spoon the mushrooms over the brioche, sprinkle with the chives, and serve immediately.

TARTE AU CHÈVRE

GOAT CHEESE TART

A goat cheese tart makes a lovely summer dish, served with a crisp green salad or a handful of peppery pink radishes, and although Fran will probably kill me for saying so, I see no shame in using store-bought pastry if its preparation seems rather excessive.

Serves 6

For the pastry shell
1⅔ cups all-purpose flour
Pinch of salt
4 tablespoons (½ stick) unsalted butter, chilled and diced
4 tablespoons vegetable shortening, chilled and diced
3 tablespoons ice-cold water, as needed

For the filling
3 tablespoons unsalted butter
3 medium leeks, white and pale green parts only, thinly sliced
⅔ cup half-and-half
2 large eggs
Sea salt, to taste
Freshly ground black pepper, to taste
5 ounces rindless goat cheese

To make the pastry shell, stir the flour and salt in a medium bowl. Add the butter and vegetable shortening and rub it together with your fingertips until the mixture resembles fine crumbs. Stir in the water with a fork until the mixture comes together. Place on a lightly floured work surface and knead briefly until the pastry is evenly blended, and shape into a disk. Wrap in plastic wrap and refrigerate for 30 minutes.

Lightly butter a 9½-inch tart pan. On a lightly floured surface, roll out the pastry about 1 inch wider than the pan's diameter. Carefully roll the pastry around the rolling pin and unroll onto the pan. Press into the pan and trim off any excess pastry with a small knife. Refrigerate for another 30 minutes.

Heat the oven to 350°F. Line the pastry with aluminum foil and fill with dried beans. Bake until the edge of the pastry looks set, about 30 minutes. Lift off the foil and beans, and bake until the pastry is barely browned, about 10 minutes more.

For the filling, melt the butter in a large skillet over medium-low heat. Add the leeks, cover, and cook until very tender, about 15 minutes. Whisk in the half-and-half and eggs, and season with salt and pepper. Pour into the pastry shell. Top with the cheese and bake until the filling sets, about 45 minutes. Serve warm or cooled to room temperature.

CHÊVRERIE

CHÈVRE CHAUD À LA GASCONNE

WARM GOAT CHEESE GASCON STYLE

This recipe is a regional version of the classic warm goat cheese salad, and provides a splendid opportunity to experiment with the wide variety of goat cheeses available in markets. As it ages, goat cheese gains in flavor but loses moisture, so for this recipe use small cheeses that are firm but not too dry. The cheese naughtily named crottins *(droppings) are best for this, rolled in ash, black pepper, or herbs for extra flavor. Fran likes pitted black olives for this dish; I prefer the jeweled, multicolor varieties that you can buy by the generous scoop in any market south of La Rochelle, gleaming with oil and heady with chiles, but you decide; it's your kitchen.*

Serves 6

A bunch of fresh basil
2 garlic cloves
¾ cup olive oil
Sea salt, to taste
Freshly ground black pepper, to taste
6 individual goat cheeses (*crottins*)
1 baguette
1 head red endive, leaves separated
1 head Belgian endive, leaves separated
½ cup pitted black or mixed olives

To make a marinade, finely chop the basil and garlic, then add the oil, salt, and pepper. Pour the marinade into a shallow dish and add the cheeses, making sure they are coated evenly. Cover and refrigerate for 24 hours.

Cut the baguette into 12 thick slices and toast. Cut the cheeses in half crosswise, arrange on a baking sheet, and grill under a hot broiler until golden; place 1 cheese on each toast. Divide the endive leaves and olives among 6 plates. Place 2 toasts on each plate, then top with the marinade.

SOUFFLÉ AU ROQUEFORT

ROQUEFORT SOUFFLÉ

Produced only in Roquefort, in the Aveyron, this is one of the oldest (and strongest!) of French cheeses. According to local legend it was discovered by accident, when a young shepherd boy left his lunch of bread and cheese in a cave and forgot it. Returning some weeks later he found that the result of his carelessness was a blue-veined dry cheese that people found strangely appetizing. Serve the soufflé with a green salad.

Serves 6

4 tablespoons unsalted butter
⅓ cup all-purpose flour
1 cup plus 2 tablespoons milk
5 ounces Roquefort, mashed
4 large eggs, separated, at room
    temperature
Freshly grated nutmeg

Heat the oven to 375°F. Butter a 6- to 7-cup soufflé dish. Melt the butter in a small saucepan over medium-low heat, remove from the heat, and whisk in the flour. Gradually whisk in the milk. Return to the heat and cook, whisking constantly, until the sauce comes to a boil and thickens. Remove from the heat. Whisk in the Roquefort, then the egg yolks and nutmeg. Beat the egg whites until stiff peaks form. Stir one-quarter of the whites into the Roquefort mixture, then add to the remaining whites and fold together. Pour into the soufflé dish. Bake in the center of the oven until puffed and golden, 35 to 40 minutes. Serve at once.

CITROUILLE AU JAMBON DE BAYONNE

PUMPKIN WITH BAYONNE HAM

This simple but striking combination of air-dried ham and sweet, tender pumpkin makes a delightful autumn dish. Don't discard the pumpkinseeds; just toast them in the oven, tossed with some olive oil and coarse salt, and add them to a green salad for a satisfying crunch.

Serves 6

1 small cooking pumpkin (2 pounds), such
   as cheese or sugar pumpkin
Sea salt, to taste
Freshly ground black pepper, to taste
12 thin slices Bayonne ham, or prosciutto
   or Serrano ham
Olive oil, as needed

Heat the oven to 375°F. Cut the pumpkin into 6 wedges and remove the seeds. Cut each wedge in half crosswise and season with salt and pepper. Wrap each in the ham. Place on a baking sheet and drizzle with oil. Bake until the pumpkin is tender and the ham is nicely crisp, 30 to 40 minutes. Serve hot.

Salads and Vegetables

Even if you're not a vegetarian, I can't see how you can fail to be seduced by the amazing selection of multicolored, multishaped fruits and vegetables, mushrooms, nuts, leaves, and herbs that can be found in markets in France. Huge fresh bunches of leaves and salads; glossy purple eggplant; red, white, yellow, even blue or black potatoes; cherries and apricots sold not by the pound but by the crate. Here, produce is definitely not uniform; many varieties are available that are not known or used in England, and for me it is one of the joys of being in an unfamiliar place to taste, test, and experiment with the unusual in all its forms. Many of these dishes can easily serve as main courses or may be prepared as accompaniments to meat or fish, as required.

Salads are one of the most creative and versatile areas of food preparation. This is fast, tasty food at its best, vibrant with colors, textures, and flavors—a perfect excuse for an impulse-buy. Hot or cold, anything goes—and for those of you who still associate the salad with iceberg lettuce and dieters' fare, think of fresh goat cheeses, rolled in herbs and toasted on brioche, served on a bed of peppery arugula with a drizzle of balsamic vinegar, or buttery avocados tossed in lime juice, or peppery pink radishes straight from the garden, or green herbs, heady with sunlight, with sliced foie gras and sweet persimmons fresh from the tree. Salads are a celebration of the best of the French market (where many of the fruit and vegetables have been picked that same morning), and at best should excite the most jaded palate with a perpetual rush of flavors.

Once prepared, salads should never be refrigerated; this kills the taste and perpetuates the "iceberg lettuce" fallacy that all salads are dull. Dressing, too, is an essential, and for the most part I like to use a simple vinaigrette—3 tablespoons of oil, 1 tablespoon of vinegar, 1 teaspoon of mustard and seasoning—although fans of creamy dressings will also find plenty in this chapter to satisfy their taste buds.

AÏOLI

This creamy garlic dressing works with a variety of dishes, including salads, crudités, and most fish dishes.

Serves 6 generously

4 garlic cloves, chopped
Sea salt, to taste
2 large egg yolks, at room temperature
2 teaspoons white wine vinegar
¾ teaspoon Dijon mustard
1½ cups olive oil
Juice of ½ lemon
Freshly ground black pepper, to taste

Pound the garlic with the salt in a mortar and pestle until smooth. Add the egg yolks, vinegar, and mustard and mix until rich and creamy. Transfer to a mixing bowl. Very slowly, whisk in the oil. Add the lemon juice and pepper. If you prefer a thinner consistency, mix in a spoonful of warm water. To store, refrigerate with plastic wrap pressed directly on the surface of the aïoli.

MAYONNAISE

Real mayonnaise is so easy to make and so much better than the store-bought variety that I wonder why anyone bothers to buy the bottled stuff at all. Use a light, mild olive oil for a subtle flavor that will not overwhelm the dish, or try using half olive oil to half vegetable oil. Serve with crudités—a selection of raw vegetables, trimmed and cut into slices—for a colorful simple apéritif.

Serves 6 generously

2 large egg yolks
2 teaspoons white wine vinegar
2 teaspoons Dijon mustard
1½ cups olive oil
Juice of ½ lemon
Sea salt, to taste
Freshly ground black pepper, to taste

Whisk the egg yolks, vinegar, and mustard together to a rich creamy consistency. Very slowly, whisk in the olive oil until the mayonnaise amalgamates. Whisk in the lemon juice, salt, and pepper. If you prefer a thinner consistency, mix in a spoonful of warm water. To store, refrigerate with plastic wrap pressed directly on the surface of the mayonnaise.

Try making your own versions by adding any of the following:

Chopped herbs: Tarragon, chervil, parsley, basil
Chopped cornichons, capers, shallots, scallions
Chopped watercress
Curry powder, mango or apricot chutney
Harissa (spicy Moroccan chile paste), cumin

ROUILLE

The beauty of this simple mayonnaise-based sauce is its versatility, although it is particularly used to enhance the flavors of salads, fish, and soup.

Serves 6 generously

1 red bell pepper, ribs and seeds discarded, chopped
1 hot red chile pepper, ribs and seeds discarded, chopped
4 garlic cloves, chopped
Sea salt, to taste
3 large egg yolks
2 teaspoons white wine vinegar
¾ teaspoon Dijon mustard
1½ cups olive oil
Juice of ½ lemon
Freshly ground black pepper, to taste

Pound the red pepper, chile, and garlic with the salt in a mortar and pestle until smooth. Add the egg yolks, vinegar, and mustard and mix until rich and creamy. Transfer to a mixing bowl. Very slowly, whisk in the oil. Add the lemon juice and pepper. If you prefer a thinner consistency, mix in a spoonful of warm water. To store, refrigerate with plastic wrap pressed directly on the surface of the rouille.

VINAIGRETTE AUX HERBES

This simple and versatile dressing is great with all vegetables, salads, grilled fish, cold pork, and chicken, and can even be added to pasta.

Serves 6

1 garlic clove, chopped
Generous bunch of mixed fresh herbs: flat-
    leaf parsley, basil, chives, tarragon
3 tablespoons red wine vinegar
2 teaspoons Dijon mustard
1 teaspoon sugar
⅔ cup olive oil
Sea salt, to taste
Freshly ground black pepper, to taste

Place the garlic in a medium bowl. Remove the leaves from the herbs and chop finely. Add to the bowl with the vinegar, mustard, and sugar and mix well. Slowly pour in the olive oil, mixing all the time with a whisk or a handheld blender. When all the oil is blended, add the salt and pepper.

SAUCE AUX NOIX

NUT SAUCE

This rich walnut dressing is excellent with crudités, toasted sourdough bread, or as a simple pasta sauce.

Serves 6

1 cup (4 ounces) walnuts
3 garlic cloves, chopped
Sea salt, to taste
Freshly ground black pepper, to taste
¾ cup walnut oil
A bunch of flat-leaf parsley, chopped

Pound the walnuts and garlic in a mortar into a fine paste (or process them in a blender). Mix in a tablespoon of warm water and season with the salt and pepper. Slowly whisk in the oil (the sauce will thicken and take on a texture similar to mayonnaise). Mix in the parsley.

SALADE DE MARMANDE

TOMATO SALAD

Marmande tomatoes are one of the highlights of the summer season, with their firm skins and intense flavor. Their irregular shapes and colors ranging from stripy yellow to fire engine red may look peculiar, but the taste is phenomenal, and they need nothing but a drizzle of olive oil and a bunch of locally grown herbs to make a terrific simple meal. In the U.S., you can find Marmande tomato seeds online for growing, but it's much easier to make the salad with a selection of heirloom tomatoes from your farmers' market.

Serves 6

3 to 4 large Marmande or heirloom
    tomatoes
A big bunch of basil and thyme
¼ cup olive oil
Sea salt, to taste
Freshly ground black pepper, to taste

Core the tomatoes and slice them finely. Remove the leaves from the basil and thyme and chop them. Place the tomatoes in a bowl. Add the olive oil and herbs and season with salt and pepper. Serve at once with crusty bread.

SALADE DE CONCOMBRE

CUCUMBER SALAD

These simple, clean flavors are perfect for a hot summer's day.

Serves 6

2 large cucumbers
A bunch of dill, chopped
¼ cup olive oil
Juice of 1 lemon
Sea salt, to taste
Freshly ground black pepper, to taste

Peel the cucumbers and slice in half lengthwise. Run the tip of a teaspoon down the middle of the cucumber halves to remove the seeds. Slice the cucumbers finely at an angle and place in a bowl. Add the dill, olive oil, and lemon juice. Season with salt and pepper. Toss well and leave to marinate for 30 minutes.

MELON AU FLOC

MELON WITH FLOC

"Melons are like men," my grandmother used to say. "You have to give them a good feel before you can be sure you've made the right choice." In this case, it means checking that your melon has a suitably intoxicating scent, is firm to the touch, and heavy in the hand. Charentais melons are small, gray-green, and stripy, with bright Halloween pumpkin–colored flesh and a sweet, musky taste. The stronger the scent, the riper the melon, and a market-ripe melon is usually best eaten on day of purchase. Slightly unripe melons should be left to ripen, if possible, on an outside window ledge in the shade. Never refrigerate melons—it kills both taste and scent—but do store them in a cool place. This is best with chilled floc (that divine and closely guarded secret of the Gascon region), but a decent port will do.

Serves 6

3 small ripe melons, preferably Charentais
1 cup chilled red floc or port

Cut a small slice from the top and bottom of each melon, making a flat base to set it on. Cut the melons through the middle, and with a dessertspoon, scoop out the seeds. Place the prepared melons on individual plates. Serve at the table, and fill each hollow with chilled floc.

SALADE DES CHAMPS DE MER

SHRIMP AND MELON SALAD

This is a salad of gentle flavors: fragrant melon, dill, and sea-fresh shrimp, balanced with a squeeze of lemon. Fran likes to use shelled shrimp for this dish, while I prefer to shell my own.

Serves 6

2 small ripe melons, preferably Charentais
1 pound large shrimp, cooked
A bunch of dill, chopped
2 tablespoons olive oil
1 lemon

Slice the top and bottom from each melon, then place upright and cut away the skin from top to bottom until the whole melon is peeled and reveals the sweet juicy flesh. Cut the melon in half lengthwise and scoop out the seeds with a dessertspoon. Slice the melon into thin wedges, and cut these in half crosswise. Arrange on a serving platter or among 6 plates, then top with the shrimp and dill. Drizzle with the olive oil and a squeeze of lemon juice. Serve immediately.

SALADE PRINTANIÈRE

SPRING SALAD WITH BACON AND EGGS

This recipe is so simple that it can only work if made with freshly picked seasonal lettuce and good organic eggs.

Serves 6

3 tablespoons red wine vinegar
1 tablespoon Dijon mustard
1 teaspoon sugar
1 garlic clove, finely chopped
9 tablespoons olive oil
6 large organic eggs
4 ounces slab bacon, rind removed, cut into thick strips
1 large head of young, tender lettuce, washed
A bunch of flat-leaf parsley, chopped
Sea salt, to taste
Freshly ground black pepper, to taste

Put the vinegar, mustard, sugar, and garlic in a jar and mix well. Add ½ cup oil, put the lid on the jar, and shake vigorously until blended. Place the eggs in a pan of warm water, bring to a boil, and simmer gently for 6 minutes. When cooked, drain them, and run cold water into the pan for 2 minutes.

   Heat the remaining tablespoon of oil in a skillet. Add the bacon and cook over medium heat until nicely crisp. Meanwhile, break the lettuce into a large bowl, add the parsley, salt, and pepper. Peel the eggs and cut them into quarters; add them to the salad and scatter with the hot bacon. Pour over the vinaigrette, toss, and serve at once.

POMMES DE TERRE EN SALADE

POTATO SALAD

Use the many different varieties of potato that are available to make this salad.

Serves 6

1½ pounds small boiling potatoes
2 tablespoons red wine vinegar
1 red onion, sliced
¾ pound small tomatoes, sliced
3 tablespoons olive oil
A bunch of celery leaves, chopped
A bunch of chives, chopped
A bunch of flat-leaf parsley, chopped
1 garlic clove, chopped
Sea salt, to taste
Freshly ground black pepper, to taste

Wash the potatoes and steam until tender, about 25 minutes. Slice while still warm and place in a bowl. Add the vinegar, toss, and leave to cool.

Just before serving, add the onion, tomatoes, olive oil, celery leaves, chives, parsley, and garlic. Toss well and season with salt and pepper.

SALADE AUX NOIX

SALAD WITH WALNUTS

This salad also works very well with a little dried goat cheese or Roquefort crumbled into the dressing.

Serves 6

4 slices country-style bread
1 or 2 garlic cloves, peeled
3 tablespoons walnut oil
3 tablespoons olive oil
2 tablespoons red wine vinegar
1 head green leaf or butter lettuce, washed
1 cup (4 ounces) walnuts, coarsely chopped
Sea salt, to taste
Freshly ground black pepper, to taste

Toast the bread and rub on both sides with the garlic. Cut into cubes, place in a bowl, drizzle with 2 tablespoons of the walnut oil and toss. Place the remaining walnut oil in a small bowl and mix with the olive oil and vinegar. Break the lettuce into a large serving bowl and scatter with the garlic toast and walnuts. Add the dressing, season with salt and pepper, toss, and serve at once.

CHÈVRE AUX FIGUES

GOAT CHEESE WITH FIGS

For a brief, magical time in midsummer, fresh figs are available in abundance all over France. These have little in common with the limp, anemic varieties we get in most supermarkets, but when you can get luscious, firm, ripe black figs, it's worth making the most of them. This dish contrasts the musky pink flesh of summer figs with rich, cured ham and the freshest of goat cheeses.

Serves 6

12 ripe figs
12 thin slices dry-cured ham, such as Bayonne ham or prosciutto
7 ounces rindless goat cheese
24 fresh mint leaves, chopped
Sea salt, to taste
Freshly ground black pepper, to taste
Olive oil, for serving

Prepare the figs by removing the stems and then cutting vertically almost to the base. Turn each fig and cut again, squeezing carefully to open up the fig. Chop the ham into ¼-inch-wide ribbons and place in a bowl. Crumble in the goat cheese, add the mint leaves, season with salt and pepper, and mix. Arrange the figs on a large plate and spoon the mixture into the open center of each fig. Drizzle with olive oil and chill for 30 minutes before serving.

AVOCAT EN SALADE

AVOCADO AND POTATO SALAD

This salad is perfect served slightly warm, on its own, or as a sophisticated accompaniment to a simple grilled chicken or fish dish.

Serves 6

1 pound small boiling potatoes, preferably purple potatoes
2 bunches chives
1 or 2 fresh hot chile peppers
A bunch of flat-leaf parsley
2 tablespoons crème fraîche
1 tablespoon olive oil
Juice of ½ lemon
Sea salt, to taste
Freshly ground black pepper, to taste
3 large ripe avocados

Steam the potatoes until tender, about 20 minutes, then cool for 10 minutes. Chop the chives, chiles (with the seeds if you like it spicy), and the leaves from the parsley and mix together in a bowl. Add the crème fraîche, olive oil, lemon juice, salt, and pepper and mix well. Just before serving, chop the potatoes and place in a serving bowl. Cut the avocados in half, remove the pits, and scoop out the flesh with a large spoon. Chop the avocado flesh into pieces, add to the potatoes, and mix. Drizzle with the dressing, toss, and serve.

SALADE TOULOUSAINE

TOULOUSE-STYLE SAUSAGE AND BEAN SALAD

This salad can be served hot or cold, but I prefer it just warm, to give the rich flavors a greater intensity. If using canned chickpeas and white beans, look for the organic ones. If using dried, soak them overnight, drain, and bring to a boil in a separate saucepan of water. Boil for 10 minutes, reduce the heat, and simmer until tender, 1 to 1½ hours.

Serves 6

4 fresh pork sausages, preferably Toulouse
    style, but Italian will do
A little olive oil, for cooking the sausages
1 cup (8 ounces) dried chickpeas, cooked,
    or 2 (19-ounce) cans, rinsed and drained
1 cup (8 ounces) dried small white beans,
    cooked, or 2 (19-ounce) cans, rinsed and
    drained
¼ cup olive oil
2 tablespoons white wine vinegar
1 tablespoon whole grain mustard
4 sage leaves, chopped
Sea salt, to taste
Freshly ground black pepper, to taste
3 ripe tomatoes, peeled and seeded

Cook the sausages in a little olive oil in a large skillet over medium heat until golden and cooked through, 15 to 20 minutes. Remove and keep warm. Place the cooked chickpeas and white beans in the same skillet, then add the olive oil, vinegar, mustard, and sage, and season with salt and pepper. Cook over medium heat, stirring often, until the beans are heated, about 5 minutes. Chop the tomatoes, add to the beans, mix well, and place in a bowl. Slice the sausages, stir into the beans, and serve hot or cooled.

SALADE TIÈDE AU CAMEMBERT

WARM SALAD WITH CAMEMBERT DRESSING

This dish relies on contrasting textures for its effect, matching the smoked bacon with spicy young leaves and a luscious Camembert dressing for a really luxurious salad.

Serves 6

1 tablespoon olive oil
6 ounces smoked bacon, rind removed,
    cut into thick sticks
9 ounces ripe Camembert, rind cut away
½ cup dry white wine
10 ounces baby spinach, washed
10 ounces boiling potatoes, cooked and
    diced
A few scallions
Sea salt, to taste
Freshly ground black pepper, to taste

Heat the oil in a skillet over medium heat. Add the bacon and cook until crisp. Place the rindless Camembert and wine in a small saucepan and heat very gently without boiling. Place the spinach and diced potatoes in a large bowl. Chop the scallions and add them, along with the salt and pepper. Whisk the melted Camembert and wine until smooth, drizzle over the salad, and top with the crispy lardons. Serve immediately.

HARICOTS EN SALADE

FAVA BEAN AND GOAT CHEESE SALAD

Spring's first fava beans are so young, sweet, and delicate that it seems hardly worthwhile making any plans for them at all—most of them will be eaten straight from the pod long before they see the inside of a cooking pot. This little salad makes the most of these most tender of beans, just dipped in boiling water and served with a young goat cheese and the simplest of dressings.

Serves 6

4¼ pounds fresh fava beans in their pods
¼ cup olive oil
2 tablespoons balsamic vinegar
Sea salt, to taste
Freshly ground black pepper, to taste
A bunch of fresh mint
4 ounces rindless goat cheese

Remove the beans from their pods. Bring a large pot of water to a boil over high heat. Add the beans and simmer for 3 minutes. Drain in a colander and rinse under cold running water until the beans are cool. Put the drained beans in a bowl and add the oil, vinegar, salt, and pepper. Remove the mint leaves from the stalks and chop the leaves. Add to the beans and mix well. Transfer to a serving bowl, crumble the goat cheese over the beans, and serve at once.

LENTILLES EN SALADE

LENTIL SALAD

Lemon, oil, and fresh herbs give a delicate summery flavor to this tomato and lentil salad, delicious on its own or as an excellent accompaniment to grilled fish or chicken.

The French town of Puy is famous for its green lentils, which are much smaller and cook more quickly than typical lentils. They are available at specialty food markets and from online sources. It's worth the effort to search them out.

Serves 6

7 ounces (about 1 cup) lentils, preferably lentilles du Puy
6 ripe large tomatoes
2 zucchini
7 ounces sorrel or spinach leaves
¼ cup olive oil
1 garlic clove, finely chopped
Juice of 1 lemon
Sea salt, to taste
Freshly ground black pepper, to taste

Cook the lentils in a saucepan of simmering water until barely tender, about 20 minutes (or longer if using regular lentils). Meanwhile, plunge the tomatoes in boiling water for a few seconds, then peel them. Roughly chop the tomatoes and place in a mixing bowl. Grate the zucchini, roughly cut the sorrel into shreds, and add to the tomatoes. Add the olive oil, garlic, lemon juice, salt, and pepper, and mix well. Drain the lentils well when cooked, add to the other vegetables, toss well, and serve warm or cooled.

SALADE D'AUTOMNE

AUTUMN SALAD

Walnuts and homegrown apples give a distinctly autumnal feel to this tasty salad—perfect for an Indian summer meal with chilled rosé.

Serves 6

1 head red leaf lettuce, washed
A bunch of chervil, chopped
A bunch of flat-leaf parsley, chopped
1 cup (4 ounces) walnuts, roughly chopped
2 tart apples
2 tablespoons cider vinegar
Juice of ½ lemon
2 tablespoons walnut oil
3 tablespoons olive oil
Sea salt, to taste
Freshly ground black pepper, to taste
14 ounces sliced smoked ham, cut into
  thin strips

Tear the lettuce into a large bowl and add the chopped chervil and parsley and the walnuts. Core and slice the apples and add to the salad. Add the vinegar, lemon juice, walnut oil, and olive oil, then the salt and pepper, and toss well. Gather the ham into small bunches and scatter over the top of the salad. Toss lightly and serve.

CAROTTES RÂPÉES AU MIEL

GRATED CARROTS WITH HONEY

A delicious way to prepare grated carrots; the result is sweet, spicy, and addictive. I'm happy to eat this on its own as a main dish, but it works well with grilled chicken or fish.

Serves 6

1½ pounds carrots
3 tablespoons clover honey
1 tablespoon white wine vinegar
1 tablespoon Asian dark sesame oil
2 teaspoons smoked paprika, such
  as pimentón de La Vera
Sea salt, to taste
Freshly ground black pepper, to taste
2 tablespoons toasted sesame seeds, a
  mixture of white and black seeds

Peel the carrots and grate them into a bowl. Mix together the honey, vinegar, sesame oil, paprika, salt, and pepper. Add to the carrots and mix well. Let stand at room temperature for 1 hour to infuse the flavors. Sprinkle with the toasted sesame seeds and serve.

POMMES DE TERRE AUX HERBES

SAUTÉED POTATOES WITH HERBS

Freshly picked herbs make all the difference to this dish. I grow my own (and anyone with a window ledge can do the same), but I find that in the warmer regions of France, most herbs are generally more strongly flavored than they are at home. Be generous with them—this dish should be almost like a salad that can be enjoyed hot or cold.

Serves 6

2 pounds boiling potatoes
¼ cup olive oil
1 shallot, finely diced
3 garlic cloves, chopped
3 sprigs of chervil, chopped
3 sprigs of flat-leaf parsley, chopped
3 sprigs of tarragon, chopped
A slim bunch of chives, chopped
Sea salt, to taste
Freshly ground black pepper, to taste

Steam the potatoes until tender, about 20 minutes. When cool enough to handle, cut into quarters. Heat the olive oil in a large skillet over medium heat. Add the potatoes and sauté on each side until golden, 10 to 12 minutes. Transfer to paper towels and pour off any excess oil. Add the shallot and garlic and cook over low heat for 2 minutes. Return the potatoes to the skillet, add the herbs, and mix well. Season with salt and pepper and serve hot, making sure to scrape all of the shallot, garlic, and herbs out of the skillet.

POMMES À L'AUVERGNATE

AUVERGNE-STYLE MASHED POTATOES WITH CHEESE

This is a traditional way of preparing potatoes from the central Auvergne region, and should be made with very young Cantal cheese (although in a pinch you can use Tomme cheeses, or any other kind of semihard variety, such as Gruyère). The result is a rich and succulent dish with a glossy, firm texture.

Serves 6

2¼ pounds baking potatoes, such as
    russet or Burbank, peeled and cut
    into chunks
2 garlic cloves, crushed and peeled
¼ cup milk
4 tablespoons (½ stick) unsalted butter
Sea salt, to taste
Freshly ground black pepper, to taste
14 ounces Cantal, shredded

Cook the potatoes and garlic in a large saucepan of boiling water until tender, about 20 minutes. Drain well. Return the potatoes to the pan and cook over low heat, shaking the pan often, to steam off the excess moisture. Remove from the heat. Mash the potatoes and garlic until very smooth (a potato ricer produces the best results). Beat in the milk, butter, salt, and pepper. Add the cheese and beat vigorously until the cheese has melted and formed a rich, elastic mixture. Serve at once.

POMMES DE TERRE AUX TRUFFES

SAUTÉED POTATOES WITH TRUFFLES

This ultraluxurious way of dressing up the humble potato relies on the earthy flavors of goose fat and truffle for the best effect. In the French southwest, where factory farming has never really managed to gain a stranglehold over the region, many farmers are now replanting truffle oaks in the place of corn and rapeseed (canola), with the result that, in season, fresh truffles are now increasingly affordable. If you can't get these, try a few wild mushrooms and a drizzle of truffle oil.

Serves 6

2 pounds boiling potatoes
About ¾ ounce truffle, whole or shavings
¼ cup rendered goose fat or olive oil
A bunch of flat-leaf parsley, chopped
Sea salt, to taste
Freshly ground black pepper, to taste
1 tablespoon truffle oil (optional)

Steam the potatoes for 20 minutes. When just cool enough to handle, cut into 1½-inch-thick slices. If using a whole truffle, slice as finely as possible; if using shavings, dice finely. Heat the goose fat (if you're a vegetarian, use a rich, fruity olive oil instead) in a large skillet over medium heat. Add the potatoes, truffle, parsley, salt, and pepper and cook, stirring often, for 5 minutes. Drizzle with the truffle oil, if using. Serve, making sure that you gather all the truffle pieces and parsley from the bottom of the skillet.

POMMES DE TERRE AUX CÈPES

SAUTÉED POTATOES WITH PORCINI

Once more, goose fat is a key ingredient in this dish, giving a wonderful richness to the crispy fried potatoes and complementing the fruity flavor of the mushrooms. Vegetarians might try walnut oil or one of the richer varieties of olive oil, as they work just as well.

Serves 6

2 pounds boiling potatoes
4 large fresh porcini or other mushrooms, cleaned
2 tablespoons goose fat or olive oil
2 garlic cloves, chopped
Sea salt, to taste
Freshly ground black pepper, to taste
A bunch of flat-leaf parsley, chopped

Steam the potatoes for 20 minutes. When just cool enough to handle, cut into 1½-inch-thick slices. Slice the porcini through the cap and stalk. Heat the goose fat in a large skillet over medium heat. Add the potatoes and porcini and cook, stirring occasionally, until the potatoes are golden, about 8 minutes. Reduce the heat to low, stir in the garlic, and cook for a minute more. Season with salt and pepper, stir in the parsley, and serve hot.

HARICOTS VARIÉS À LA CIBOULETTE

Simple spring vegetables make a delightful accompaniment to roast spring lamb, steamed fish, or creamy gratin dauphinois.

Serves 6

Choose 1¾ pounds in total from a selection
 of the following vegetables: fava beans
 (shelled), peas, thin green beans, wax
 beans, snow peas, sugar snap peas
A bunch of mint
A large bunch of chives
6 tablespoons (¾ stick) unsalted butter
Sea salt, to taste
Freshly ground black pepper, to taste

Bring a large pot of water to a boil over high
heat, then add the vegetables and cook just
until bright green, about 3 minutes. Drain well.
Strip the mint leaves from the stems and chop
finely, along with the chives. Melt the butter in
a large skillet over medium heat. Add the
drained vegetables and the mint and chives to
the skillet and season with the salt and pepper.
Toss well and serve hot.

ARTICHAUTS AU VIN BLANC

ARTICHOKES IN WHITE WINE

Young, sweet artichokes are one of the delights of early summer. This recipe keeps their shapes more or less intact, but adds white wine, herbs, and butter for a luxurious treatment. Small, new season artichokes are best for this recipe. If using larger ones, increase the cooking time and test by inserting a thin knife into the middle (they should be soft when cooked).

Serves 6

12 small artichokes
A bunch of flat-leaf parsley, chopped
12 sprigs of thyme
3 garlic cloves, chopped
6 tablespoons olive oil
Sea salt, to taste
Freshly ground black pepper, to taste
1 cup dry white wine
6 tablespoons (¾ stick) unsalted butter

Heat the oven to 325°F. Cut off the stalk from the base of each artichoke and pull off the tough outer leaves. Cut the tops off about halfway down. Using a teaspoon, scrape out the inner choke. Stand the artichokes up in a flameproof casserole. Add equal amounts of the parsley, thyme, garlic, and oil to the center of each artichoke and season with salt and pepper. Pour in the white wine and cover tightly with aluminum foil, being sure to make a tight seal. Bake until tender, about 35 minutes.

Transfer the artichokes to 6 shallow bowls. Bring the cooking liquid in the casserole to a boil over high heat. Add the butter and cook until the liquid is reduced by half. Spoon into the center of each artichoke and serve with crusty bread.

PETITES COURGETTES FARCIES

SMALL STUFFED ZUCCHINI

Fran and I love the shapes and colors of these beautiful little tubby summer squash. When young, they have a dense texture, which holds its shape well when cooked, and a sweet, delicate flavor that contrasts nicely with the smoked bacon. If you're vegetarian, omit the bacon, and compensate accordingly with a generous scatter of sea salt, which will enhance the subtle taste.

Serves 6

6 round zucchini, available in season at
    farmers' markets
2 tablespoons olive oil
½ pound slab bacon, rind removed, cut into
    ½-inch dice
4 shallots, finely chopped
3 garlic cloves, chopped
A bunch of marjoram leaves, chopped
Zest and juice from 1 unwaxed lemon
Sea salt, to taste
Freshly ground black pepper, to taste

Heat the oven to 350°F. Cut a lid from the stem end of each zucchini. Use a teaspoon to scoop out the flesh, leaving shells about ½ inch thick; dice the zucchini flesh and place in a bowl. Heat the oil in a medium skillet over medium heat, add the bacon, and cook until lightly browned, about 5 minutes. Add the shallots and garlic and cook for 2 minutes more. Mix into the zucchini, along with the marjoram, lemon zest and juice, salt, and pepper. Fill the zucchini with the mixture. Place on a lightly oiled baking sheet and top with their lids. Bake until tender, about 45 minutes.

POIVRONS FARCIS

STUFFED RED PEPPERS

Here is a fine excuse to wander a summer market in search of the plumpest, the ripest, the most colorful selection of vegetables. Fat peppers, gleaming eggplant, exotically patterned zucchini and tomatoes—these ingredients are a joy to handle and to look at as well as to eat, so you can afford to be as lavish and creative as you like.

2 red onions
2 medium eggplant
2 zucchini
6 tablespoons olive oil, plus extra for
　drizzling
6 red bell peppers
4 large tomatoes, chopped
1 fresh hot red chile pepper, seeded and
　chopped
3 garlic cloves, chopped
3 sprigs of thyme, leaves only
Sea salt, to taste
Freshly ground black pepper, to taste

Heat the oven to 350°F. Chop the onions, eggplant, and zucchini into 1-inch dice. Place in a large baking dish and toss with 6 tablespoons olive oil. Bake the vegetables, stirring halfway through cooking, until they begin to soften, about 30 minutes.

Meanwhile, cut the red peppers in half lengthwise and remove the seeds. Mix the tomatoes, chile pepper, and garlic in a bowl and mix in the par-cooked vegetables. Stir in the thyme leaves and season with salt and pepper. Place the red peppers cut side up on an oiled baking sheet and generously fill with the vegetable mixture. Drizzle with a little olive oil and bake until the vegetables are meltingly tender, about 1 hour more.

NAVETS AU VIN BLANC

TURNIPS IN WHITE WINE

This recipe calls for small, tender young turnips that can be cooked whole to preserve their natural sweetness.

Serves 6

1½ pounds small turnips
2 tablespoons unsalted butter
1½ tablespoons sugar
¼ cup dry white wine
A bunch of flat-leaf parsley, chopped
Sea salt, to taste
Freshly ground black pepper, to taste

Wash and scrub the turnips. Place in a wide saucepan with the butter and sugar and add just enough cold water to cover the turnips. (If you are using larger turnips, cut them into wedges first.) Bring to a boil over high heat. Reduce the heat to medium-low and simmer, stirring occasionally, until the turnips are tender, about 20 minutes, adding a bit more water if necessary to keep them covered. Add the wine and parsley, season with salt and pepper, and bring to a simmer. Serve hot.

AUBERGINE AU GRATIN

ROASTED EGGPLANT
CASSEROLE

The irresistible texture and glossy sheen of fresh, plump eggplant is always enough to tempt me into buying. Fran suggests this as an accompaniment to roast lamb, and it's also substantial enough to eat on its own.

Serves 6

2 garlic cloves, peeled
6 tablespoons olive oil
1 large eggplant (1⅓ pounds), trimmed
1¾ pounds ripe tomatoes
4 sprigs of thyme, leaves only
Sea salt, to taste
Freshly ground black pepper, to taste
½ cup vegetable stock

Heat the oven to 350°F. Rub an earthenware baking dish (about 10 inches square) with 1 garlic clove and 1 tablespoon oil. Chop the remaining garlic. Slice the eggplant and tomatoes about ½ inch thick. Put all the vegetable ends in the bottom of the dish and arrange the remaining slices in alternate layers, seasoning with the thyme leaves, salt, and pepper as you go. Pour over the stock and drizzle with the remaining oil. Bake for 45 minutes. Reduce the heat to 325°F and bake until the vegetables are tender, about 45 minutes more. Serve hot or cooled.

CAROTTES AUX POIREAUX

ROASTED CARROTS
WITH LEEKS

The method used for this dish of carrots and leeks gives them a very tender, silky consistency, and the white wine infuses the carrots with a flavor that will increase as the dish is reheated.

Serves 6

6 medium carrots, trimmed
5 leeks, white and pale green parts only
6 tablespoons (¾ stick) unsalted butter
1 shallot, chopped
2 garlic cloves, chopped
2 sprigs of thyme
2 bay leaves
1¼ cups dry white wine
Sea salt, to taste
Freshly ground black pepper, to taste

Heat the oven to 400°F. Cut the carrots in half lengthwise. Cut the leeks into 2-inch lengths. Melt the butter in a roasting pan over medium heat. Add the shallot and garlic and cook until softened, about 1 minute. Add the carrots and leeks, along with the thyme and bay leaves. Stir well to coat with butter and cook for 2 minutes. Add the wine and season with salt and pepper. Roast until the vegetables are tender, about 30 minutes. Remove the thyme and bay leaves and serve at once or reheat to serve later.

BETTES DU VIGNERON

VINEYARD-STYLE SWISS CHARD

It's difficult to resist huge colorful bunches of chard with their white or red stems and big, dark green leaves. Chard is more commonly cooked in water, but I find this dilutes its flavor. In this dish, the method of quick preparation keeps the flavor and color intact and gives the chard a firm, meaty texture.

Serves 6

3 pounds Swiss chard, well washed
2 tablespoons olive oil
1 medium onion, chopped
1 garlic clove, chopped
Sea salt, to taste
Freshly ground black pepper, to taste
⅔ cup raisins
½ cup pine nuts, toasted
Juice of ½ lemon

Pull the leaves from the chard stems. Chop the leaves roughly and set aside. Peel the strings away from the lengths of stems (as with celery), and chop the stems into 2-inch lengths. Heat the oil in a large skillet over medium heat, add the onion and the stems, then sauté for 5 minutes. Add the chard leaves, garlic, salt, and pepper. Cook over high heat, stirring constantly. Add the raisins and pine nuts, squeeze in the lemon juice, and mix well. Serve hot.

BROCCOLI AUX ANCHOIS

BROCCOLI WITH ANCHOVIES

*Quick steaming ensures that none of the bright color
and firm texture of the broccoli is lost; and the
anchovies and lemon juice just add enough of a
contrast to enhance, rather than overwhelm,
the delicate flavor.*

Serves 6

3 ounces salted anchovy fillets
1 large head broccoli, cut into florets
4 tablespoons olive oil, as needed
Zest and juice of 1 unwaxed lemon
1 fresh red chile, finely chopped
Sea salt, to taste
Freshly ground black pepper, to taste

Soak the anchovies in warm water to remove
some of the saltiness, about 10 minutes. Drain
carefully and pat dry. Cut the fillets into thin
lengths and set aside. Steam the broccoli
until bright green and barely tender, about
4 minutes. Mix the anchovies, olive oil, lemon
zest and juice, chile, salt, and pepper in a
serving bowl. Add the broccoli and mix well.
Serve hot.

LÉGUMES RÔTIS SUR PETITS TOASTS

ROASTED VEGETABLES WITH GARLIC TOASTS

This colorful and adaptable vegetarian dish works equally well hot or cold, as a snack, a starter, or a main course with salad. The trick to this dish is in the efficient cooking of all the vegetables. The oven must be hot so that they roast quickly and retain their individual textures and colors.

Serves 6

2 onions
3 zucchini
2 red bell peppers, cored
2 medium eggplant
4 tablespoons olive oil
6 slices sourdough bread
2 garlic cloves, peeled
Sea salt, to taste
Freshly ground black pepper, to taste

Heat the oven to 400°F. Cut the onions into wedges and the zucchini, red peppers, and eggplant into roughly 1½-inch chunks. Put in a large roasting pan and coat with the oil. Roast for 25 minutes, stir well, and continue roasting until tender, about 10 minutes more. Meanwhile, toast the sourdough bread and rub with the garlic. Season the vegetables with salt and pepper and serve with the warm garlic toasts on the side.

POIREAUX AU POIVRON ROUGE

LEEKS WITH RED PEPPERS

The balsamic vinegar adds just a touch of spicy sweetness to the subtly flavored and colored vegetables. Great with steamed or baked fish, chicken, or with a main course baked potato dish.

Serves 6

3 red bell peppers
4 leeks, white and pale green parts only
1 tablespoon olive oil
1 cup vegetable stock
A sprig of rosemary
1 or 2 garlic cloves, chopped
2 tablespoons balsamic vinegar
1 teaspoon sugar

Cut the peppers in half, remove the stems and seeds, and chop roughly. Cut the leeks into 2-inch chunks. Heat the oil in a large saucepan over high heat. Add the vegetables and sauté for 5 minutes, stirring often. Add the stock, rosemary, and garlic and cover. Reduce the heat to medium-low and simmer for 5 minutes. Uncover, return the heat to high, and boil until the liquid has almost completely evaporated. Stir in the balsamic vinegar and sugar and serve at once.

CITROUILLE AU ROMARIN

ROASTED PUMPKIN
WITH ROSEMARY

It's great to have a reason to buy a pumpkin other than to make Halloween lanterns. I grow these myself—they look great in the vegetable patch— but markets sell excellent ones in season. Smaller pumpkins taste sweeter and have firm, luminous orange flesh (look for the sugar or cheese varieties), but I avoid the very large ones that tend toward stringiness. Vegetarians can omit the bacon; just add a little extra seasoning to compensate, or a dash of red chili oil at the end.

Serves 6

1 small cooking pumpkin (about 2 pounds)
4 tablespoons olive oil, plus a little extra
   for the roasting pan
4 sprigs of rosemary
½ pound slab bacon, rind removed, cut into
   thick strips
Sea salt, to taste
Freshly ground black pepper, to taste

Heat the oven to 400°F. Wash the pumpkin skin, then cut the pumpkin into chunks about 2 inches square. (Do not discard the seeds— they are delicious roasted.) Place the pumpkin in a large bowl and toss with the oil. Strip the rosemary leaves from the stalks, chop finely, and add to the pumpkin, along with the bacon, salt, and pepper, and toss again. Oil a large roasting pan and heat the empty pan in the oven for 5 minutes. Add the pumpkin mixture and roast until the pumpkin is tender, about 30 minutes. Serve at once.

FENOUIL RÔTI

ROAST FENNEL

Roasting the fennel gives it an irresistible sweetness without destroying its fresh and subtle aniseed taste. For best results, and to ensure that the fennel cooks evenly, use a large ovenproof dish and arrange the fennel pieces in a single layer.

Serves 6

6 tablespoons (¾ stick) unsalted butter
2 or 3 fennel bulbs, trimmed
1 cup vegetable stock
⅓ cup packed light brown sugar
2 tablespoons white wine vinegar
5 sprigs of thyme

Heat the oven to 375°F. Melt the butter in a large flameproof roasting pan over medium-high heat. Cut the fennel into quarters or halves, depending on the size, and cook in the butter on both sides until golden, about 3 minutes per side. Add the stock, brown sugar, vinegar, and thyme and bring to a boil. Bake until the fennel is tender, about 25 minutes. Serve at once.

LENTILLES DU PUY

WINE-BRAISED PUY LENTILS

*Unique Puy lentils (see page 73) are by far the best
kind of lentils for this slow-cooking dish. Dark
in color and plump in consistency, they retain and
intensify the rich flavors of the wine and herbs,
with a result that can be enjoyed on its own or
as a perfect accompaniment to roast pork.*

Serves 6

¼ cup olive oil
2 red onions, sliced
2 garlic cloves, chopped
2 cups Puy lentils or brown lentils
2 cups hearty red wine
1 (14½-ounce) can chopped tomatoes
   in juice
2 bay leaves
4 sprigs of oregano
2 sprigs of rosemary
Sea salt, to taste
Freshly ground black pepper, to taste

Heat the oven to 350°F. Heat the oil in a Dutch
oven over medium heat. Add the onions and
garlic and cook for 5 minutes. Add the lentils,
wine, tomatoes, ¾ cup water, bay leaves,
oregano, rosemary, salt, and pepper and bring
to a boil. Bake for 30 minutes. Stir, then
continue baking until the lentils are tender
and the liquid has evaporated away, leaving the
lentils to absorb the rich flavor, about
30 minutes more.

TOURTE AU CAMEMBERT

POTATO, CABBAGE, AND CAMEMBERT CASSEROLE

A lovely combination of fresh seasonal vegetables, floury potato, and golden, creamy Camembert topping makes an excellent vegetarian main course for a miserable winter's day.

1½ pounds all-purpose potatoes, such as
   Yukon gold
¼ head cabbage, cored and chopped
1 large egg, beaten
1 or 2 fresh hot green chiles, seeded and
   chopped
1 garlic clove, chopped
Sea salt, to taste
Freshly ground black pepper, to taste
5 tablespoons olive oil
½ pound cherry tomatoes
6 ounces Camembert, sliced

Heat the oven to 350°F. Boil the potatoes in a saucepan of boiling water for 15 minutes. Drain, and when cool enough to handle, cut into 1½-inch cubes. Mix the potatoes, cabbage, egg, chiles, garlic, salt, and pepper in a bowl. Oil a metal baking dish with some of the oil, and place the dish in the oven to heat for a few minutes. Add the remaining oil to the vegetables and mix. Remove the hot dish from the oven and fill with the potato mixture. Scatter the tomatoes over, then top with the cheese slices. Bake until the vegetables are golden, about 45 minutes.

Fish

We had to move slightly further afield for these fish recipes, to Aveyron and the Atlantic coast, which, though only a couple of hours' drive away from the Baïse, already demonstrates a completely different set of culinary traditions. This intense gastronomic regionalization is one of the joys of rural France, and to truly appreciate its diversity you need to embrace wholeheartedly the various specialties of each region. To choose to eat steak in Aveyron would be as perverse as to try to buy fish in Nérac. The markets reflect this: all Fran and I had to do to collect our fish recipes was to visit them, talk to the locals, and allow temptation to have its way.

Freshly caught fish is essential for these recipes, so make sure you choose fish with bright eyes, shiny, colorful scales, and no strong odor. Good, fresh fish should always feel firm and have bright red, healthy gills. Your fishmonger should be able to gut and fillet any fish for you, but if you prefer to do the job yourself, ensure your filleting knife is as sharp as possible. Keep your fish in the coolest part of the fridge under damp paper, and always cook it on the day of purchase.

FRUITS DE MER À L'AÏOLI

ROASTED SHELLFISH
WITH AÏOLI

The only skill involved in creating this spectacular and sociable dish is that of choosing the freshest and most delicious local ingredients. We've used razor clams here, which are abundant on the Atlantic coast, and palourdes, a generous-sized mollusk with a characteristic hazelnut flavor. You can afford to be flexible, however—and remember that if you choose what's in season and what has been caught locally, you can't go wrong. Serve with a green salad.

Serves 6

2 pounds palourdes or cherrystone
    clams
6 razor clams or 12 mussels
1 pound large shrimp, preferably with
    heads
6 crab claws
6 sea scallops
¼ cup olive oil
3 garlic cloves, chopped
2 fresh hot chile peppers, seeded and
    chopped
3 sprigs of rosemary
A bunch of flat-leaf parsley
A bunch of basil
Sea salt, to taste
Freshly ground black pepper, to taste
Aïoli (page 52)

Place the palourdes and razor clams in a large bowl of cold water and soak for 10 minutes. Scrub the shells, rinse, and repeat; this removes any sand from the shells.

Heat the oven to 400°F. Place the palourdes, razor clams, shrimp, crab, and scallops in a large bowl. Add the oil, garlic, and chiles. Strip the rosemary leaves from the twigs, chop the leaves, and add them to the shellfish. Toss well, then pour into a large roasting pan. Roast for 15 minutes, checking halfway through that everything is cooking evenly (if not, move things around in the pan).

Strip the leaves from the parsley and basil and chop. Sprinkle the shellfish with the herbs, season with salt and pepper, and serve with the aïoli.

BOUQUET AU CITRON ET CITRON VERT

BOILED SHRIMP WITH LEMON AND LIME

This is such a simple dish that it hardly counts as a recipe at all, though it's still my all-time favorite seaside picnic dish. In France, cooked prawns are available at roadside stalls all down the coast, of course, but nothing beats the freshest, sweetest Atlantic prawns, served with lemon and lime, and a glass of chilled Muscadet.

Serves 6

4½ pounds large shrimp, preferably with heads
3 lemons, cut into wedges
3 limes, cut into wedges

Bring a large pot of water to a rapid boil over high heat. Add the shrimp. Return to the boil and cover. Cook until all of the shrimp turn bright pink or orange, about 2 minutes. Drain and rinse under cold running water. Refrigerate in a colander on a rimmed baking sheet to catch the drips until chilled, at least 2 hours. Serve chilled with the lemon and lime wedges.

OYSTERS AUX LARDONS

OYSTERS WITH BACON

Having been brought up on raw oysters (where my family comes from, it's considered sacrilege to eat oysters any other way), I was at first rather suspicious of this dish. Having tried it, however, I have to say that it's pretty good. Just don't tell my mother!

Serves 6

36 oysters
12 slices bacon, finely chopped
A bunch of flat-leaf parsley, leaves chopped
3 garlic cloves, chopped
Freshly ground black pepper, to taste

Open the oysters with an oyster knife. Heat a broiler until very hot. Place the oysters in their shells on a broiler pan. Do not overcrowd the pan—it is best to cook and serve the oysters in batches, if necessary. Mix together the bacon, parsley, and garlic in a bowl and season with the pepper. Divide among the oysters, sprinkling over the top. Place under the broiler and cook until the oyster juices are bubbling and the bacon is sizzling, 3 to 4 minutes. Serve at once.

SEICHE FARCIE

STUFFED SQUID

This recipe is a specialty of Sète, a beautiful village on the Mediterranean with canals running through it. Use medium or large squid (seiche in French) for this unusual combination of sea and land ingredients.

Serves 6

12 squid without tentacles (about 1 pound total weight)
6 tablespoons olive oil
½ pound ground pork
2 garlic cloves, chopped
¾ cup fresh bread crumbs
⅓ cup shelled pistachios, chopped
A bunch of flat-leaf parsley, leaves finely chopped
A bunch of oregano, leaves finely chopped
Sea salt, to taste
Freshly ground black pepper, to taste
1 large egg
¾ cup dry white wine

Check that the squid have been properly cleaned and have no thin transparent film on them or shards of cartilage inside the sacs. Heat 2 tablespoons oil in a medium skillet over medium heat. Add the pork and garlic and cook, breaking up the meat with a spoon, until the pork loses its pink color, about 5 minutes. Remove from the heat and add the bread crumbs, pistachios, parsley, oregano, salt, and pepper. Mix well. Beat the egg and add to the mixture, stirring through until the mixture combines.

Using a small spoon, stuff each squid, taking care not to overfill. Leave about 1 inch free at the open end of each squid to allow the stuffing to expand. Heat the remaining 4 tablespoons oil in a large skillet over medium-high heat. Fry the squid on all sides until golden brown, about 8 minutes. Transfer to a platter and cover to keep warm. Add the wine to the pan, bring to a boil, and cook until reduced by half. Pour over the squid and serve at once.

VILLE DE LÈGE - CAP FERRET

La Pointe est fragile,
aidez-nous à la protéger !

SALADE DE CALAMARS

SQUID SALAD

This warm squid salad is quick and easy to make. Prepared fresh, the squid is creamy and tender on the inside, golden and crispy on the outside, and is irresistible served hot over the zesty dressed salad.

Serves 6

1 unwaxed lemon
1 head green lettuce, washed
5 ounces arugula, washed
6 tablespoons olive oil
Sea salt, to taste
Freshly ground black pepper, to taste
A bunch of fresh parsley, leaves finely chopped
A bunch of lemon thyme, leaves finely chopped
2 garlic cloves, finely chopped
1½ pounds small squid, cleaned

Grate the zest and squeeze the juice from the lemon. Break the lettuce into pieces in a large bowl and add the arugula. Mix ¼ cup olive oil, lemon juice, salt, and pepper in a small bowl. Combine the parsley, thyme, lemon zest, and garlic in another bowl.

Check that the squid have been properly cleaned and have no thin transparent film on them. Cut off the tentacles and cut the body into ¼-inch-wide rings. Heat the remaining oil in a large skillet over high heat until very hot. Add the squid rings and tentacles and cook, stirring constantly, for 1 minute. Add the garlic mixture and cook until the squid is barely opaque, about 1 minute more.

Toss the salad and lemon dressing together. Add the hot squid and serve at once.

SALADE DE CRABE À L'AVOCAT

AVOCADOS WITH CRAB SALAD

This delicious combination of sweet crab and creamy avocado is perfect for a summer picnic or light lunch. Purists may prefer to cook their own crab, but most fishmongers have cooked, shelled crabmeat. Do not even think of making this with canned crabmeat.

Serves 6

2 pounds crabmeat, picked over for shells and cartilage
3 scallions, finely sliced
1 fresh hot red chile pepper, chopped
Juice of 2 limes
¾ pound cherry or grape tomatoes
3 tablespoons olive oil
2 tablespoons sesame seeds, toasted
Sea salt, to taste
Freshly ground black pepper, to taste
1 small head Boston or butter lettuce, washed
3 ripe avocados

Mix the crabmeat, scallions, chile, and lime juice in a medium bowl. Cut the tomatoes in half lengthwise and place in another bowl, along with the oil and sesame seeds. Season with the salt and pepper. Separate the lettuce leaves and divide among 6 plates. Cut each avocado in half lengthwise and remove the pits. Peel the avocados and place 1 on each plate. Generously fill the avocados with the crab salad, then spoon the tomato salad on the side. Serve at once.

SOLE VAPEUR

STEAMED SOLE WITH
SPRING VEGETABLES

The chervil in the lemon-and-oil dressing gives the steamed sole a distinctive, unusual, aromatic freshness.

Serves 6

A bunch of chives
A bunch of chervil
⅓ cup plus 1 tablespoon olive oil
Zest and juice of 2 unwaxed lemons
Sea salt, to taste
Freshly ground black pepper, to taste
6 (5-ounce) sole fillets
6 baby leeks
4 ounces asparagus, trimmed
4 ounces sugar snap peas
1 cup shelled fava beans

Chop the chives and chervil leaves. Mix with the oil, lemon zest and juice, salt, and pepper. Oil a steamer insert, place in a large pot filled with water (but not touching the steamer), and bring to a boil over high heat. Roll up the fillets lengthwise into neat logs and place in the steamer, making sure that the final fold is underneath to keep them rolled while cooking. Top with the leeks. Steam for 3 minutes. Add the asparagus, sugar snap peas, and fava beans and cook until the fillets are opaque, about 2 minutes more. Carefully transfer the sole and vegetables to plates. Serve at once with the herbed oil spooned over the fish.

BARBUE AU THYM

BROILED BRILL
WITH THYME

This simple recipe makes the most of a delicious sea fish without overpowering its taste. In France, the Atlantic denizen barbue *(brill) would be the first choice for this broiled treatment; elsewhere use a firm-fleshed but delicately flavored whitefish such as turbot or halibut steaks. Enjoy with a salad or a few steamed vegetables for the authentic taste of the French seaside.*

Serves 6

6 (7-ounce) turbot or halibut steaks
A bunch of thyme
¼ cup olive oil
Zest of 1 unwaxed lemon
1 garlic clove, chopped
Sea salt, to taste
Freshly ground black pepper, to taste

Dry the fish steaks with paper towels. Pick all the thyme leaves off the twigs and chop finely. Mix the thyme with the olive oil, lemon zest, garlic, salt, and pepper in a glass or ceramic dish large enough to hold the fish. Add the fish to the lemon marinade and turn to coat the fish all over. Cover and marinate for an hour or so in the refrigerator. When ready to cook, heat the broiler to high and oil the broiler rack. Place the fish on the rack and broil until the fish turns opaque, about 4 minutes per side. Serve at once.

MAQUEREAU À LA DIJONNAISE

ROASTED MACKEREL
WITH DIJON MUSTARD

Gleaming, fresh blue mackerel are one of the Atlantic's greatest treasures, prepared here with young leeks and Dijon mustard for a subtle combination of flavors and textures.

Serves 6

6 mackerels, filleted
Sea salt, to taste
Freshly ground black pepper, to taste
2 tablespoons Dijon mustard
A bunch of oregano, leaves chopped
Olive oil, for drizzling
2 small, thin leeks
1 teaspoon coriander seeds, crushed

Place a rack in the top third of the oven and heat the oven to 400°F. Score the skin of the mackerel fillets with a sharp knife and season with the salt and pepper. Turn the fillets over, spread the flesh with the mustard, and sprinkle with the oregano.

Oil a roasting pan and arrange six of the fillets on it, skin side down. Trim and thinly slice the leeks, and place on the fillets. Sprinkle with the coriander seeds and season the leeks with salt and pepper. Place the remaining fillets on top of the fillets in the pan, sandwich style. Drizzle with a little oil. Roast in the top third of the oven until the fillets are opaque, about 12 minutes. Serve at once.

MULLET AU POIVRON ROUGE

SAUTÉED MULLET WITH RED PEPPERS

There are only a few fish at the French market as beautiful and enticing as the red mullet. (In the U.S., you're most likely to find fresh mullet in Gulf Coast markets, but there are substitutes.) This recipe spices it up with chiles and sweet red peppers for a simple but elegant light meal.

Serves 6

4 tablespoons olive oil
2 red onions, sliced
2 red bell peppers, seeded and cut into strips
1 fresh hot red chile, seeded and chopped
3 garlic cloves, chopped
¼ cup fish stock
1 tablespoon white wine vinegar
¾ cup all-purpose flour
Sea salt, to taste
Freshly ground black pepper, to taste
6 (5-ounce) red mullet, pompano, or sea bass fillets

Heat 2 tablespoons oil in a skillet over medium-high heat. Add the red onions and bell peppers and cook for 5 minutes. Add the chile and garlic and cook for 2 minutes more, taking care not to burn the garlic. Stir in the stock and vinegar, reduce the heat to medium-low, and cook until the peppers are tender, about 10 minutes.

Meanwhile, spread the flour on a plate and season with salt and pepper. Dip the fillets in the flour and shake off any excess flour. Heat the remaining 2 tablespoons oil in a large skillet over high heat. Add the fish and cook until golden, about 3 minutes per side. Serve at once with the peppers.

SAUMON AU CHAMPAGNE

SALMON WITH CHAMPAGNE SAUCE

This is a spectacular celebratory dish, perfect for using up that last glass of flat champagne (or a perfect excuse for opening up another bottle). It's easy to make, too, which means that you can dazzle your guests with your conversation as well as your cooking.

Serves 6

3 tablespoons unsalted butter
3 shallots, finely chopped
6 (6-ounce) salmon steaks
1⅔ cups champagne or sparkling white wine
⅓ cup heavy cream
Sea salt, to taste
Freshly ground black pepper, to taste
A bunch of dill, fronds chopped

Melt the butter in a large skillet over medium heat. Add the shallots and cook until softened, about 3 minutes. Arrange the salmon over the shallots in a single layer. Add the champagne and bring to a simmer. Cover and simmer until the salmon looks opaque, about 8 minutes. Transfer the salmon to a platter and cover with aluminum foil to keep warm. On high heat, boil the cooking liquid until it has reduced by half. Add the cream and boil until the sauce is thick enough to coat a wooden spoon. Season with salt and pepper and stir in the dill. Serve the salmon with the sauce spooned over the top.

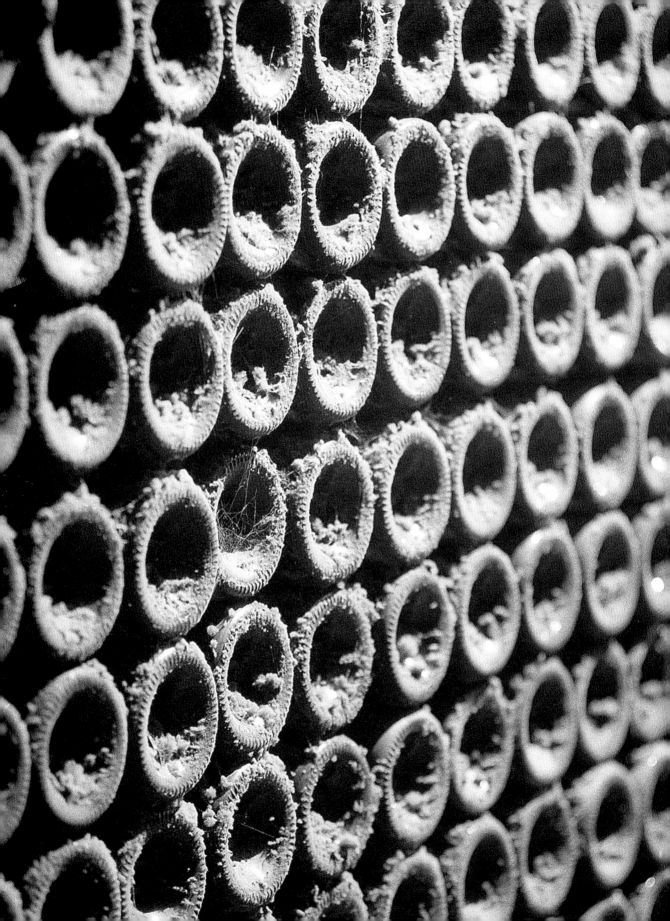

DAURADE AU VIN BLANC

SEA BREAM WITH WHITE WINE AND VEGETABLES

This dish relies principally on the freshness of the ingredients, and the white wine infuses the young vegetables with a heady yet delicate flavor. Daurade is a beloved Mediterranean fish; the porgy is a close North American relative.

Serves 6

6 (6-ounce) sea bream, porgy, or sea bass fillets
1 pound baby carrots with greens, trimmed and peeled
1¼ cups dry white wine, plus more if needed
6 sprigs of thyme
2 bay leaves
½ cup olive oil
1 pound asparagus, trimmed
¾ cup shelled green peas (from 12 ounces peas in the pod)
Sea salt, to taste
Freshly ground black pepper, to taste

Heat the oven to 425°F. Remove excess bones from the fish with tweezers. Dry the fish with paper towels (to help get a golden color) and score the skin with a sharp knife to keep the fish from curling while cooking.

Place the carrots, wine, thyme, and bay leaves in a large roasting pan. Cover tightly with its lid or a sheet of aluminum foil. Bake for 15 minutes.

Meanwhile, heat ¼ cup of the oil in a large skillet over medium-high heat until very hot. In batches, add the fish, skin side down, and cook just until seared, about 1 minute. Turn and sear for 1 minute more. Keep the pan hot so the fish seals quickly. As soon as all the fish is seared, take the carrots from the oven and add the fish, skin side up. Add a bit more wine if it has boiled away. Add the asparagus and peas and drizzle with the remaining ¼ cup oil. Baste the fish and vegetables with the pan juices. Return to the oven without a cover and roast until the fish looks opaque, about 7 minutes more. Season with salt and pepper and serve at once.

TRUITE DE MER SAUCE VERTE

SEA TROUT WITH
GREEN SAUCE

*The fresh green sauce complements the grilled sea
trout perfectly in this tangy summer dish.
Serve with hot pappardelle and roasted half
tomatoes.*

Serves 6

6 (5-ounce) sea trout fillets, patted dry
    with paper towels
4 ounces pitted green olives
2 tablespoons white wine vinegar
2 tablespoons capers, drained and rinsed
A bunch of flat-leaf parsley, leaves only
A bunch of tarragon, leaves only
Juice of 1 lemon
6 tablespoons olive oil, plus more if needed
Freshly ground black pepper, to taste

Heat the broiler until hot and oil the broiler
rack. Score the fillet skins with a sharp knife.
Grill the fish, skin side up, for 5 minutes. Turn
and cook until the fish looks opaque, about 2
minutes more. While the fish broils, make the
sauce: Process the olives, vinegar, capers,
parsley, tarragon, and lemon juice in a blender.
Add enough oil to make a thick paste. Season
with pepper. Serve the fish at once with the
sauce.

TURBOT AUX CREVETTES ROSES

ROASTED TURBOT WITH PINK SHRIMP

In his Grand Dictionnaire de Cuisine, *Dumas maintains that the combination of turbot and shrimp is a typically English dish—all I can say is that the French must have taken it back without anyone noticing.*

Serves 6

¼ cup olive oil

6 (6- to 7-ounce) turbot steaks, patted dry with paper towels

3 sprigs of thyme

3 bay leaves

Sea salt, to taste

Freshly ground black pepper, to taste

6 tablespoons unsalted butter

6 extra-large shrimp, in their shells

4 ounces large shrimp, shelled and deveined

Juice of 2 lemons

A bunch of flat-leaf parsley, leaves chopped

Heat the oven to 425°F. Pour the oil into a large roasting pan. Add the turbot, thyme, and bay leaves and season with salt and pepper. Roast until the fish looks opaque, about 15 minutes. Meanwhile, melt the butter in a large skillet over medium heat. Add the extra-large unshelled shrimp and cook just until they turn pink, about 4 minutes. Remove from the pan and reserve, leaving the butter in the skillet. Add the shelled shrimp to the skillet and cook until they turn pink, about 2 minutes. Add the lemon juice and parsley. Pour the shrimp into the roasting pan over the turbot, top each with a reserved shrimp, and serve at once.

TRUITE À L'ÉTOUFFÉE

"SMOTHERED" TROUT

This is the perfect way to prevent trout from losing its tenderness in the oven, and it can be adapted for almost any fish (red snapper, sea trout, sea bass, and so on). The variations are endless—try experimenting with other herbs or capers, or by adding large shrimp and a spoonful of crème fraîche.

Serves 6

6 sheets aluminum foil, about 15 inches
    long
12 small red-skinned potatoes, cooked
    and sliced
2 leeks, white and green parts only,
    chopped and washed
2 shallots, finely chopped
2 garlic cloves, chopped
Sea salt, to taste
Freshly ground black pepper, to taste
6 trout, cleaned
½ cup dry white wine
4 tablespoons (½ stick) unsalted butter,
    cut into 6 slices
6 sprigs of thyme
1 lemon, cut into 6 wedges

Heat the oven to 400°F. For each parcel, place a foil sheet on the work surface. Place one-sixth of the potatoes on the bottom half of the foil. Mix the leeks, shallots, and garlic in a bowl and season with the salt and pepper. Spoon one-sixth of the leek mixture over the potatoes. Add 1 trout, about 1½ tablespoons wine, a slice of butter, and a sprig of thyme. Fold the foil and tightly crimp the edges closed. Place the parcels on baking sheets. Bake for 20 minutes. Serve with lemon wedges, allowing each person to open their own parcel.

THON AUX DEUX HARICOTS

TUNA WITH TWO BEANS

*The melting consistency of flageolet beans makes a
lovely contrast to the barely cooked, crisp green
beans and just-seared tuna steaks.*

Serves 6

6 (6-ounce) tuna steaks
8 ounces thin green beans (haricots
  verts), trimmed
1 (14-ounce) can flageolet beans, drained
  and rinsed, or use 1 (15-ounce) can
  small white beans
4 ounces pitted green olives
4 ripe tomatoes, peeled, seeds removed,
  chopped
A bunch of basil, leaves stripped from
  stalks
3 tablespoons olive oil
Zest and juice of 1 unwaxed lemon
1 garlic clove, chopped
Sea salt, to taste
Freshly ground black pepper, to taste

Bring a large saucepan of water to a boil. Heat a
ridged skillet over high heat until very hot. In
batches, sear the tuna on both sides: 2 minutes
per side for rare, 3 minutes for medium,
4 minutes for well done.

Meanwhile, add the green beans to the
water and cook until bright green, about
2 minutes. Add the drained beans, reduce the
heat to low, and cook to heat through, about
1 minute. Drain well. Return the two beans to
the saucepan. Add the olives, tomatoes, basil,
oil, lemon zest and juice, and garlic and
season with salt and pepper. Toss well over low
heat until heated. Divide the bean mixture
among 6 dinner plates, top each with a tuna
steak, and serve at once.

SAINT-JACQUES AUX POMMES VAPEUR

SEARED SCALLOPS WITH STEAMED POTATOES

This rustic combination of sautéed sea scallops, bacon, and steamed tarragon potatoes is typical of the Southwest coast, where farmers and fishermen exchange recipes as well as tall tales.

Serves 6

1½ pounds small boiling potatoes
3 tablespoons olive oil
7 ounces slab bacon, rind removed, cut into thick strips
1 tablespoon white wine vinegar
A bunch of tarragon, leaves chopped
Sea salt, to taste
Freshly ground black pepper, to taste
18 large sea scallops
3 tablespoons unsalted butter

Steam the potatoes until tender, about 20 minutes. Meanwhile, heat 1 tablespoon oil in a large skillet over medium-high heat. Add the bacon and cook until crisp, about 6 minutes. Transfer the bacon to paper towels to drain. When the potatoes are tender, cool until easy to handle, and slice them into thick rounds. Mix the sliced potatoes, bacon, the remaining 2 tablespoons oil, vinegar, and tarragon (reserve a bit for the garnish in a bowl), and season with salt and pepper.

Rinse the scallops and pat dry on paper towels. Heat the butter in a very large skillet over medium-high heat. Add the scallops and cook until golden, about 1 minute per side. Divide the warm salad among 6 dinner plates. Top each with 3 scallops, sprinkle with the reserved tarragon, and serve at once.

Serves 6

2 pounds monkfish
Sea salt, to taste
Freshly ground black pepper, to taste
½ cup all-purpose flour
3 tablespoons unsalted butter
2 tablespoons olive oil
14 ounces chanterelles, cleaned
2 shallots, chopped
2 garlic cloves, chopped
¾ cup dry white wine
⅓ cup heavy cream
A bunch of flat-leaf parsley, leaves chopped

Remove all of the membrane from the monkfish (this is important, otherwise cooking will turn it an unpleasant gray). Cut the two fillets away from the central bone, then divide the flesh into 6 equal pieces. Season the monkfish with the salt and pepper and roll it in the flour, shaking off any excess flour. Heat the butter and oil in a large skillet over medium-high heat. Add the fish and sear for 1 minute on each side. Remove the fish. Add the chanterelles, shallots, and garlic to the skillet. Reduce the heat to low and cook, stirring often, for 5 minutes. Return the fish to the skillet, increase the heat to medium, add the wine, and cover. Simmer for 5 minutes. Uncover and cook over high heat to reduce the liquid by half. Add the cream and cook until the liquid thickens slightly, about 2 minutes. Stir in the parsley and serve at once.

LOTTE AUX GIROLLES

MONKFISH WITH CHANTERELLES

This is a complex, luscious marriage of flavors, rich with cream, wine, and fragrant chanterelle mushrooms. Serve the monkfish with something appropriately gentle: plain rice, steamed potatoes, or simple pasta shells.

FLÉTAN À LA BORDELAISE

HALIBUT IN BORDEAUX-STYLE RED WINE SAUCE

Serves 6

14 ounces pearl onions
3 tablespoons unsalted butter
14 ounces button mushrooms
1 (750 ml) bottle dry red wine, preferably
   Bordeaux
2 sprigs of thyme
2 bay leaves
Sea salt, to taste
Freshly ground black pepper, to taste
6 (7-ounce) halibut steaks
2 teaspoons arrowroot dissolved in
   1 tablespoon water
A bunch of flat-leaf parsley, leaves finely
   chopped

Plunge the pearl onions into a pot of boiling water for a few moments; drain, rinse under cold water, and peel the onions. Melt the butter in a large skillet over medium heat. Add the mushrooms and onions and sauté for 5 minutes. Add the wine, thyme, bay leaves, salt, and pepper and simmer for 5 minutes. Place the halibut in the skillet, baste with the wine, cover and cook until the central bone can be easily pulled from a steak, about 6 minutes. Using a slotted spatula, transfer the fish to a platter, then use a slotted spoon to transfer the vegetables to the same platter; cover with foil to keep warm. Discard the thyme and bay leaves. Whisk the arrowroot into the skillet and cook just until the sauce thickens. Stir in the parsley. For each serving, place a halibut steak and some vegetables in a shallow bowl, spoon the sauce over, and serve at once.

Meat, Game, and Poultry

For these recipes, you should consider making friends with your local organic butcher. There's really no comparison between free-range meat and the factory-produced variety, in either taste or quality. In rural French markets of the southwest, dominated as they are by specialty farmers, most meat is free range and organic, and locals will usually point you in the direction of the best producers.

Because of the regional nature of this cookbook, you'll find that there is a greater than usual number of recipes involving game birds and poultry—pigeon, pheasant, goose, and, most especially, duck. These are freely available in French markets of the southwest, and can be found at specialist butchers in Britain. Ducks and geese in France are most commonly sold as follows:

Canard: a duck, aged 2–4 months.
Cane/canette: a female duck. In his *Grand Dictionnaire de Cuisine*, Dumas makes the point that these usually have a superior taste and tenderness to the male.

Caneton: a duckling.
Magret de canard: the breast of a duck that has been traditionally fattened for foie gras. Often smoked or air-dried, when it may be carved thinly without cooking and served as part of a salad.
Confit d'oie/de canard: a preserve of goose or duck in its own fat.
Gésiers confits: duck or goose necks in *confit*, often used in salads.
Graisse d'oie/de canard: goose or duck fat, used for enriching soups and casseroles as well as for roasting potatoes.
Foie gras: liver from a traditionally fattened goose or duck.

At the market in Nérac we were lucky enough to run into Bernard Mounet, whose family have been keeping geese and ducks for generations. Foie gras is his passion, and although his farm is small, he has won many international prizes for his produce. He was pleasantly surprised at our interest in his farm. Many English, he said, are anti-foie gras; this is because they are used to factory farming, where the birds are treated badly and without respect. On his farm, as on most other small farms of the region, the birds are fed on nothing but maize and are allowed to wander freely, and the difference is not only in the taste. You have to respect the bird, says M. Mounet, to appreciate what you are eating and where it comes from.

This idea of respect and appreciation is one that lives on in farms around the region. It forms a part of the *patrimoine*— that strange French word that implies at the same time tradition, heritage, love of the land, awareness of the past. It is a love of the *patrimoine* that has kept so many of these old country recipes alive, along with the way of life that created them. All are best using organically and preferably locally farmed meat of the highest possible quality.

AGNEAU AUX HARICOTS BLANCS

BRAISED LAMB WITH WHITE BEANS

This is a dish of strong, hearty flavors, in which the red wine, garlic, rosemary, and chiles lift the mild flavor of the white beans for a warm and delicious combination. Serve with a simple green leaf salad. My great-grandmother used to make her version of this dish every year at Easter; I'm glad to see that in Gascony, too, the tradition continues.

Serves 6

14 ounces dried white kidney (cannellini)
    beans, soaked in cold water overnight
¼ cup olive oil
1 (4-pound) leg of lamb
3 red onions, chopped
16 garlic cloves, chopped
1 (750 ml) bottle hearty red wine
2 (28-ounce) cans chopped tomatoes
¼ cup lamb, beef, or chicken stock
3 sprigs of rosemary
1 or 2 fresh hot red chiles, seeded and
    diced
Sea salt, to taste
Freshly ground black pepper, to taste

Drain the beans and place in a large saucepan. Cover with cold water and bring to a boil over high heat. Reduce the heat to medium-low and simmer for 1 hour, skimming off any foam that rises to the surface.

Heat the oven to 350°F. Heat the oil in a large flameproof casserole over medium-high heat. Add the lamb and cook on all sides until golden, about 15 minutes. Transfer to a plate. Add the onions to the pot and cook until softened, about 5 minutes. Add the garlic and cook for 1 minute more. Stir in the beans, wine, tomatoes, stock, rosemary, and chile, then season with salt and pepper. Return the lamb to the pot. Cook, uncovered, checking occasionally to be sure that the liquid hasn't boiled away and adding water as needed, until the beans are tender, about 1½ hours.
Serve hot.

BOEUF BOURGUIGNON

This is one of the best-known and most typical of French dishes, and relies on a lengthy cooking time to absorb the flavor of the herbs and wine and to give the beef an irresistible tenderness.

Serves 6

¼ cup olive oil
3 pounds beef chuck, cut into 1½-inch cubes
2 onions, chopped
2 garlic cloves, chopped
⅓ cup plus 1 tablespoon all-purpose flour
1 (750 ml) bottle red wine, preferably Burgundy
1¼ cups beef stock
1 tablespoon tomato paste
2 sprigs of thyme
2 bay leaves
Sea salt, to taste
Freshly ground black pepper, to taste
7 ounces slab bacon, rind removed, cut into thick strips
9 ounces boiling onions, peeled
9 ounces white mushrooms
A bunch of flat-leaf parsley, leaves chopped
Sliced crusty bread, sautéed in olive oil until golden, for garnish (optional)

Heat the oven to 350°F. Heat the oil in a large flameproof casserole over medium-high heat. In batches without crowding, add just enough meat to cover the bottom of the pot and brown all over, about 5 minutes per batch. Transfer the meat to a plate. Add the onions and cook until softened, about 4 minutes. Add the garlic and cook for another minute. Off the heat, sift the flour over the vegetables, and mix well. Return the pot to low heat. Gradually stir in the red wine and stock, then the tomato paste, thyme, bay leaves, salt, and pepper. Return the heat to medium-high and bring to a boil. Return the meat to the pot and cover. Bake for 2 hours.

Cook the bacon in a large nonstick pan over medium-high heat until it gives off its fat, about 5 minutes. Add the boiling onions and mushrooms and cook until the vegetables are golden, about 10 minutes. Stir into the pot and continue baking until the beef is tender, about 30 minutes more. Sprinkle with the parsley. Serve hot, garnished with the croutons, if desired.

AGNEAU FARCI

STUFFED SADDLE OF LAMB

The roasted red peppers give a smoky sweetness to the lamb in this spectacular and colorful celebratory dish.

Serves 6 to 8

1 (3½-pound) boned saddle of lamb
2 red bell peppers
2 tablespoons olive oil, plus extra for
    the pan
2 red onions, chopped
2 garlic cloves, chopped
1 (14-ounce) can artichoke bottoms,
    chopped
4 ounces ground lamb
3 ounces pitted black olives, chopped
2 sprigs of rosemary, leaves chopped
1 large egg yolk
Sea salt, to taste
Freshly ground black pepper, to taste

Heat the oven to 375°F. Lay the lamb out flat, skin side down, and have some kitchen twine ready for tying. Spear each of the red peppers with a carving fork. Turn over a gas flame (or outdoor grill) until the skin is charred and blistered. Place in a bowl, cover with plastic wrap, and let stand for 10 minutes.

Heat the oil in a large skillet over medium heat. Add the onions and cook until softened, about 5 minutes. Add the garlic and cook for 1 minute more. Mix the onions and garlic with the artichokes, ground lamb, olives, rosemary, egg yolk, salt, and pepper. Peel the red peppers, then cut the flesh away from the ribs, discarding the seeds.

Spread the artichoke mixture evenly over the lamb. Place all the red peppers in one strip down the middle. Roll the two sides of the lamb together and tie securely with string at 1-inch intervals. Lightly oil a roasting pan and add the lamb. Roast for 1 hour and 20 minutes for rare (130°F on a meat thermometer). Remove from the oven and let stand in a warm place for 20 minutes. Carve and serve.

BOEUF À LA BLONDE

BRAISED BEEF WITH BLONDE ALE SAUCE

The beer in this savory recipe gives the beef a pleasantly bittersweet edge.

Serves 6

¼ cup olive oil
3 pounds beef chuck, cut into 1½-inch cubes
3 onions, coarsely chopped
7 ounces slab bacon, rind removed, cut into thick sticks
2 garlic cloves, chopped
2 tablespoons all-purpose flour
2 cups light ale
2 sprigs of thyme
2 bay leaves
Sea salt, to taste
Freshly ground black pepper, to taste

Heat the oven to 325°F. Heat the oil in a large ovenproof casserole over high heat. In batches without crowding, add just enough meat to cover the bottom of the pot and brown the meat on all sides, about 5 minutes. Transfer to a plate. Add the onions and bacon and cook until the onions soften, about 4 minutes. Add the garlic and cook for 1 minute more. Remove from the heat and sift in the flour, stirring well. Return the pot to the heat, stir in the ale, and bring to a boil. Return the beef to the pot, stir well, and return the sauce to a boil. Add the thyme and bay leaves and season with salt and pepper. Cover tightly. Bake until the beef is tender, about 2 hours. Remove the thyme and bay leaves before serving.

PORC AUX CHÂTAIGNES

PORK WITH CHESTNUTS

Traditionally made with wild boar, this is a classic winter dish: satisfyingly sweet and starchy, but full of rich flavor. It's a terrific excuse to buy the fat, glossy new chestnuts as they begin to appear in the markets all over France (even better to collect them wild), although vacuum-packed or canned chestnuts are a godsend to anyone in a hurry.

Serves 6

3 tablespoons olive oil
1 (3-pound) boneless pork loin roast
12 ounces boiling onions, peeled
4 garlic cloves, chopped
1½ cups dry white wine
6 sprigs of fresh thyme
1 bay leaf
Sea salt, to taste
Freshly ground black pepper, to taste
30 peeled chestnuts

Heat the oven to 350°F. Heat the oil in a large ovenproof casserole over high heat. Add the pork and brown all over, about 5 minutes. Transfer to a plate. Add the onions and brown over medium heat, about 5 minutes, then stir in the garlic. Return the pork to the pot, and stir in the wine, thyme, bay leaf, salt, and pepper. Bring to a boil over high heat and cook for 3 minutes. Cover and bake for 1 hour. Add the chestnuts, return to the oven, and bake until a meat thermometer inserted in the center of the roast reads 150°F, about 30 minutes. Remove the thyme and bay leaf. To serve, carve the meat, arrange on a bed of onions and chestnuts, and serve with the sauce.

PORC AUX PRUNEAUX

GRILLED PORK CHOPS WITH PRUNE-APPLE SAUCE

This is a quick and easy cold-weather dish that makes full use of the hearty flavors of sizzling pork, winter apples, and luscious Agen prunes.

3 tart apples, peeled, cored, and sliced
7 ounces Agen prunes, pitted
¾ cup dry white wine or chicken stock
2 tablespoons Armagnac or brandy
A bunch of sage, leaves chopped
Olive oil, for sautéing
3 red onions, cut in half lengthwise and
   peeled
6 center-cut, bone-in pork chops, cut ¾ to
   1 inch thick
Sea salt, to taste
Freshly ground black pepper, to taste

Bring the apples, prunes, and wine to a boil in a medium saucepan. Cook over medium-low heat, stirring often, until the apples form a thick sauce, about 15 minutes. Stir in the Armagnac and sage and keep warm.

Meanwhile, preheat the broiler. Heat the oil in a large skillet over medium heat. Add the onions, flat side down, and brown for 8 minutes, then turn and cook, keeping the halves intact, until the onions are tender, about 8 minutes more. While the onions cook, season the pork with salt and pepper and broil until there is no sign of pink when pierced near the bone, about 10 minutes per side. Serve the chops with the sauce and onions.

FOIE GRAS AUX CHANTERELLES

No regional French cookbook is complete without a recipe for foie gras, an ingredient that goes back to Roman times and encompasses a thousand years of French culinary history. It is an artisanal product, both expensive and difficult to manufacture. This recipe is as simple as it gets, because when you're eating something this good, you need nothing more.

Serves 6

6 tablespoons unsalted butter
½ pound chanterelle mushrooms, cleaned
Sea salt, to taste
Freshly ground black pepper, to taste
1¼ pounds fresh foie gras, cut on a slight
   diagonal into six ½-inch-thick slices
6 slices brioche, toasted

Heat 3 tablespoons butter in a large skillet over high heat. Add the mushrooms and cook until browned and tender, about 5 minutes. Season with salt and pepper. Meanwhile, heat the remaining 3 tablespoons butter in a large nonstick skillet over high heat. Add the foie gras and sear for 1 minute on each side. Place 1 toasted brioche on each of 6 plates, top with the chanterelles and a piece of foie gras, and serve at once.

PORC AUX CÈPES

PORK WITH PORCINI MUSHROOMS

Cèpes (porcini) are one of the delights of the late-summer market (you're most likely to find them in the U.S. in select produce markets during autumn—in a pinch, substitute portobello mushrooms). This recipe for pork with cèpes is simple but effective; try it with some green beans for a quick, elegant meal on an autumn evening.

Serves 6

4 tablespoons olive oil
6 (¾ inch thick) boneless pork chops
4 large porcini mushrooms, cleaned and
   sliced through the caps and stalks
3 garlic cloves, chopped
¼ cup plus 2 tablespoons white wine
   vinegar
Sea salt, to taste
Freshly ground black pepper, to taste
A bunch of flat-leaf parsley, leaves chopped

Heat 2 tablespoons oil in a large skillet over medium-high heat. Sear the pork chops for 3 minutes on each side. Reduce the heat to medium-low and cook until no sign of pink shows when pierced, about 8 minutes more. Meanwhile, in another skillet, heat the remaining 2 tablespoons oil over high heat. Add the porcini and cook for 4 minutes, then reduce the heat to medium-low and cook until tender, about 10 minutes more. Stir in the garlic. Add the porcini and vinegar to the pork chops and cook for 5 minutes. Season with salt and pepper, stir in the parsley, and serve.

FOIE-GRAS
A LA FERME
CONSERVES
FOIES GRAS
CONFITS
CANARDS-GRAS
ENTIERS OU
DECOUPES
50.m.

CASSOULET TOULOUSAIN

This traditional peasant dish has a thousand variants, every one of which is considered by its followers to be the real deal. I prefer it without the bread crumbs (although I know that in some parts of France this makes me a philistine), and there is also some serious division of opinion regarding the tomatoes. Everyone agrees, however, that as winter comfort food goes, you can't get much better. The slow cooking time means that everything is infused with the rich flavors of the confit and herbs, and that the beans are lusciously soft and buttery. Enjoy it with fresh country bread, a contrasting side salad, or simply, luxuriously, on its own.

Serves 8 to 12

1 pound dried white kidney (cannellini) beans, soaked overnight in cold water, drained

8 ounces fresh pork rind

3 onions, 1 studded with 3 whole cloves

2 carrots, scrubbed, trimmed, but whole

5 large ripe tomatoes, peeled and quartered

1 bouquet garni (6 parsley sprigs, 2 bay leaves, and 1 celery stalk tied with kitchen twine)

6 garlic cloves, crushed and peeled

2 tablespoons rendered goose fat (from the confit)

1 pound boneless lamb shoulder, cut into large cubes

10 ounces fresh pork belly, cut into large cubes

Several sprigs of thyme

Sea salt, to taste

Freshly ground black pepper, to taste

1 pound goose or duck confit (page 178 or use store-bought confit)

1 pound fresh pork sausages

3 cups fresh bread crumbs

Put the beans in a large pot with the pork rind, clove-studded onion, carrots, tomatoes, bouquet garni, and 2 garlic cloves. Cover generously with cold water. Bring to a boil over high heat, reduce the heat to low, and simmer until the beans are tender, about 2 hours. Skim any foam that rises to the surface during cooking, and add more water if needed.

About 1 hour into the beans' cooking time, finely chop the remaining 2 onions and 3 of the garlic cloves. Heat 1 tablespoon of the goose fat in a large saucepan over medium-high heat. In batches, add the lamb and brown on all sides, about 8 minutes. Transfer the lamb to a plate. Add the pork belly, chopped onions and garlic, thyme, salt, and pepper to the fat in the pot. Return the lamb to the pot, cover with some of the cooking liquid from the beans, and bring to a boil; cook for 50 minutes.

Meanwhile, heat the remaining 1 tablespoon goose fat in a large skillet. Add the confit to the skillet and brown, about 5 minutes. Remove from the skillet; set aside. Add the sausages to the skillet and brown, about 5 minutes. Add the sausages to the lamb during the last 10 minutes of the lamb cooking time.

Heat the oven to 350°F. Discard the pork rind, carrots, and onion from the beans. Rub a very large, deep flameproof baking dish (preferably earthenware) with the final garlic clove. Spoon half of the beans with their cooking liquid into the dish. Top with the lamb, pork belly, and sausage mixture, including their vegetables and cooking juices, and then the confit. Cover with the remaining beans.

Bring to a boil over medium-low heat. Lightly sprinkle the top with some of the bread crumbs. Bake uncovered until the juices thicken, about 1½ hours, stirring every 20 minutes or so before sprinkling once more with bread crumbs. Leave the last bread crumb topping to form a golden crust. Let the cassoulet stand for 15 minutes before serving.

LAPIN AUX PRUNEAUX D'AGEN

RABBIT WITH AGEN PRUNES

Rabbit remains a staple ingredient in the Southwest, where hunting game has been a way of life for many centuries. This recipe, with fat, dark prunes from the town of Agen, relies on slow, gentle cooking to release the contrasting flavors. If you don't have Agen prunes, use the largest, moistest prunes you can find, preferably from a natural foods market.

3 pounds rabbit, cut into serving pieces
24 Agen prunes or large California dried plums
2½ cups red wine
2 tablespoons olive oil
5 ounces slab bacon, rind removed, cut into thick sticks
24 boiling onions, peeled
2 celery ribs, chopped
2 garlic cloves, chopped
3 tablespoons all-purpose flour
2 cups red wine
2 sprigs of thyme
1 bay leaf
Sea salt, to taste
Freshly ground black pepper, to taste
⅓ cup brandy or Armagnac

Put the rabbit and prunes in separate dishes, add half of the wine to each, and refrigerate overnight. Drain, reserving the wine.

Heat the oil in a Dutch oven over medium heat. Add the bacon and cook until browned, about 5 minutes. Use a slotted spoon to transfer the bacon to a platter. In batches, add the rabbit to the pot, and cook until browned on all sides, about 7 minutes, and transfer to the platter. Add the onions to the fat in the pot and cook until browned, about 10 minutes, and transfer to the platter. Add the celery and garlic to the pot and cook over medium-low heat until the celery softens, about 5 minutes. Sprinkle in the flour and stir well. Gradually whisk in the red wine. Return the bacon, rabbit, and onions to the pot, along with the thyme and bay leaf. Season with salt and pepper. Cover tightly and simmer gently for 1 hour.

Stir in the prunes and brandy, and cook until the rabbit is tender, about 40 minutes more. Remove the thyme and bay leaf. Serve hot.

PIGEON AU FLOC

SQUAB WITH FLOC

Most markets in the Southwest region sell pigeons, which roast well and have a dark, slightly gamey flavor. You won't find pigeon labeled as such in most markets, as its more common culinary name is squab. Substitute poussin, or small chickens, if you can't find squab. This recipe combines the roast bird with the earthy taste of morels in season and a dash of floc—that utterly addictive Gascon mixture of fresh grape juice and Armagnac—for a sweet, luscious autumn dish.

Serves 6

Olive oil, as needed
6 squab or poussin
Sea salt, to taste
Freshly ground black pepper, to taste
6 bay leaves
10 tablespoons (1¼ sticks) unsalted
    butter, at room temperature
1 pound fresh morels, shiitakes, or other
    mushrooms, cleaned
2 garlic cloves, chopped
¾ cup red floc de Gascogne or red wine
Chopped chives, for garnish (optional)

Heat the oven to 400°F. Lightly oil a shallow roasting pan. Season the squab with salt and pepper and place a bay leaf in each. Smear a tablespoon of the butter over the breast of each squab. Place on the roasting pan. Roast for 30 minutes, basting occasionally with the pan juices. The squab will be rare to medium-rare.

Heat the remaining 4 tablespoons butter in a large skillet over medium heat. Add the morels and cook until tender, about 15 minutes, taking care not to break the mushrooms when you stir them because they look beautiful if they can retain their shapes. Stir in the garlic during the last 3 minutes of cooking. When the squab are cooked, transfer them to a platter and cover with aluminum foil to keep warm. Drain the cooking juices from the pan into the mushrooms. Add the floc and bring to a boil over high heat. Boil until the liquid reduces by half, about 5 minutes.

Serve the squab on a bed of mushrooms, topped with the sauce and garnished with chives, if you like.

PERDRIX AUX PRUNEAUX

PARTRIDGES WITH POTATO-PRUNE STUFFING

Agen prunes have little in common with the small, miserable little prunes available in many markets. These are plump, dark, and heady, and work particularly well with the darker, sweeter meat of small birds such as partridge and squab.

Serves 6

6 partridges, with giblets
2 onions, chopped
2 carrots, chopped
1 sprig of thyme
1 bay leaf

Stuffing
2 medium all-purpose potatoes, such as
    Yukon gold, cooked and chopped
5 ounces Agen prunes, coarsely chopped
2 garlic cloves, chopped
Sea salt, to taste
Freshly ground black pepper, to taste
2 tablespoons unsalted butter
6 bacon slices, cut in half crosswise
3 tablespoons all-purpose flour
¾ cup red wine
1 tablespoon red currant jelly

Remove the giblets from the partridges. Combine the giblets, onions, carrots, thyme, and bay leaf in a medium saucepan and add enough cold water to cover by 1 inch. Bring to a boil and cover. Reduce the heat to low, and simmer for 45 minutes. Strain the giblet stock and set aside.

Meanwhile, heat the oven to 375°F. For the stuffing, mix the potatoes, prunes, and garlic and season with salt and pepper and use to fill the partridges. Rub the breasts with the butter, season with salt and pepper, and lay 2 bacon pieces over each partridge. Place in a shallow roasting pan. Bake for 15 minutes. Remove the bacon and set aside. Bake the partridges for 15 minutes more; they will be rare to medium-rare. Transfer to a platter and tent with aluminum foil to keep warm.

Place the roasting pan over medium heat. Whisk the flour into the pan juices and gradually whisk in the stock. Bring to a boil, then add the wine and jelly. Simmer until lightly thickened, about 4 minutes, then season with salt and pepper. Strain the sauce. Serve the partridges with the bacon and sauce.

CHEVREUIL AUX BAIES ROUGES

VENISON WITH RED BERRY SAUCE

Sweetness complements game very well, and rarely more so than in this intensely flavored late-summer dish. The berry sauce is sticky and tart, though not enough to overpower the venison's characteristic taste.

Serves 6

2 cups red wine
1 teaspoon black peppercorns, crushed
4 juniper berries, crushed
2 garlic cloves, chopped
1 bay leaf
2 pounds venison loin roast, tied
Sea salt, to taste
Freshly ground black pepper, to taste
2 tablespoons olive oil
1 tablespoon red wine vinegar
1 tablespoon packed light brown sugar
1 teaspoon arrowroot, dissolved in
    1 tablespoon water
8 ounces mixed fresh or frozen red
    berries, such as raspberries and red
    currants

Mix the red wine, peppercorns, juniper berries, garlic, and bay leaf in a glass or ceramic bowl. Add the venison. Refrigerate, occasionally turning the venison, overnight.

Heat the oven to 350°F. Remove the meat from the marinade and pat dry with paper towels. Strain the marinade into a medium saucepan and cook over medium heat until it reduces by half; set aside. Season the meat with salt and pepper.

Heat the oil in a flameproof roasting pan over medium-high heat. Add the venison and brown on all sides, about 6 minutes. Bake for about 30 minutes for rare (130°F on a meat thermometer).

Transfer the roast to a platter, tent with aluminum foil to keep warm, and let stand 10 minutes. Pour any pan juices from the roasting pan into the reduced wine, along with the vinegar and brown sugar. Bring to a boil and stir in the dissolved arrowroot. Add the berries and cook over low heat until the sauce thickens lightly, about 2 minutes. Carve the venison and serve with the sauce.

CANARD À L'ORANGE

ROAST DUCK WITH ORANGE SAUCE

This classic combination of crispy roast duck and tangy orange is difficult to beat at any time of the year, but as a winter dish, with roast potatoes or honeyed parsnips, it is truly spectacular.

Serves 4

2 tablespoons unsalted butter
2 carrots, chopped
2 onions, chopped
2 celery ribs, chopped
2 sprigs of thyme
2 bay leaves
1 (5½- to 6-pound) duck, with giblets
Sea salt, to taste
Freshly ground black pepper, to taste
4 unwaxed oranges
1 unwaxed lemon
1 tablespoon arrowroot dissolved in
    2 tablespoons water
2 tablespoons orange-flavored liqueur,
    preferably Grand Marnier
2 tablespoons sugar, preferably turbinado
1 tablespoon cider vinegar

Heat the oven to 400°F. Butter a roasting pan with 1 tablespoon butter. Add the chopped carrots, onions, celery, thyme, and bay leaves. Season the duck with salt and pepper and place on the vegetables. Cover the pan with foil and bake for 1 hour. Remove the foil and cook until the duck is golden brown, about 30 minutes more.

Meanwhile, bring the giblets and 2 cups water to a boil in a small saucepan over high heat. Reduce the heat to low, cover, and simmer for 30 minutes. Strain the stock.

Zest and juice 2 oranges and the lemon. Cut the remaining 2 oranges into wedges. Butter a small roasting pan with the remaining tablespoon butter, add the oranges, and roast on another rack in the oven during the last 20 minutes of the duck roasting time.

Transfer the duck to a platter and tent with aluminum foil to keep warm. Cook the vegetables in the pan over medium-high heat until they are nicely browned, about 5 minutes. Carefully drain off the duck fat from the pan without disturbing the sediment, reserving the fat for another use. Add 1½ cups stock to the pan and simmer for 5 minutes. On very low heat, whisk enough of the dissolved arrowroot into the pan to thicken the sauce. Strain the sauce into a medium saucepan. Stir in the orange and lemon zest and juices, liqueur, sugar, and vinegar. Cook over low heat until hot, but do not boil. Add the orange wedges to the platter. Carve the duck and serve with the oranges and sauce.

MAGRET À L'ORANGE

SAUTÉED DUCK BREAST WITH ORANGE-VEGETABLE SLAW

This is a summery version of the old classic, using chile and fennel to spice up a sweet vegetable salad. Duck breasts should never be overcooked (I prefer mine to be just seared, so that the fat is crisp and sizzling); and, in this case, the dish is best left to cool for a few minutes to allow the flavors time to develop.

Serves 6

6 boneless duck breast halves
Zest and juice from 2 unwaxed oranges
2 hot fresh chiles, diced (with seeds if you
    like the heat)
4 tablespoons olive oil
1 fennel bulb, cut into matchsticks
3 carrots, cut into matchsticks
4 celery ribs, cut into matchsticks
2 red bell peppers, seeds and ribs removed,
    cut into matchsticks
2 garlic cloves, chopped
Sea salt, to taste
Freshly ground black pepper, to taste

Using a sharp knife, score the skin of each duck breast in a close crisscross pattern. Mix the orange zest and juice, chiles, and 2 tablespoons oil in a glass or ceramic bowl. Add the duck breasts, turn to coat in the marinade, cover and let stand for 1 hour.

Heat the remaining 2 tablespoons oil in a large skillet over medium-high heat. Remove the duck from the marinade, reserving the marinade. In batches, add the duck to the skillet, skin side down. Cook for 5 minutes, then reduce the heat to medium-low, and cook until the skin is deep golden brown, about 8 minutes more. Remove excess fat from the pan. Turn and cook until the underside is browned, about 6 minutes (the duck will be medium-rare). Transfer the breasts to a carving board and tent with foil to keep warm. Pour the fat from the skillet without disturbing the sediment. Add the marinade to the skillet and bring slowly to a simmer.

Mix the fennel, carrots, celery, red peppers, and garlic in a large bowl. Add the hot marinade, mix well, and season with salt and pepper. Mound equal amounts of the slaw onto 6 serving plates. Thinly carve the breasts and top each serving with a sliced breast.

MAGRETS AUX NAVETS

DUCK BREASTS WITH TURNIPS

This time-honored combination of duck breast, smoky-sweet shallots, and fresh young turnips works very well as a warming winter dish.

Serves 6

6 boneless duck breast halves
Sea salt, to taste
Freshly ground black pepper, to taste
2 tablespoons rendered goose or duck fat
  or olive oil
24 whole shallots, peeled
14 ounces small turnips, sliced
3 tablespoons all-purpose flour
1½ cups dry white wine
1 tablespoon packed light brown sugar
2 sprigs of thyme
2 bay leaves
⅓ cup Madeira

Score the duck skin with a sharp knife in a close crisscross pattern. Season with salt and pepper. Heat 1 tablespoon fat in a large skillet over medium-high heat. Add the duck, skin side down, and cook until the skin is golden brown, about 5 minutes. Turn and cook just until browned, about 3 minutes. Transfer the duck to a plate. Without disturbing the sediment in the skillet, pour off all but 3 tablespoons of the fat; set the skillet aside.

Meanwhile, heat the remaining tablespoon of fat in another large skillet over medium heat. Add the shallots and turnips and cook until golden, about 10 minutes. Add the duck to the vegetables, reduce the heat to low, and continue cooking while making the sauce. Whisk the flour into the fat in the duck skillet to make a smooth roux. Gradually whisk in the wine. Return the skillet to medium heat and bring to a boil, whisking often. Add the sugar, thyme, and bay leaves. Pour over the duck and vegetables. Simmer until the vegetables are tender, about 8 minutes. Just before serving, remove the thyme and bay leaves and stir in the Madeira.

RILLETTES DE CANARD

This is the best way to use leftover duck, and it's still the most delicious sandwich filling I know. Serve it with lots of crusty bread and a green salad.

Serves 2

1 roast duck carcass or 2 roast duck legs
¾ cup dry white wine
Sea salt, to taste
Freshly ground black pepper, to taste
1 garlic clove, chopped
1 pinch of ground allspice
1 sprig of thyme
1 bay leaf

Chop the duck into manageable pieces and place in a heavy bottomed, medium saucepan. Add all of the remaining ingredients plus ⅓ cup water. Cover tightly. Simmer over low heat, stirring frequently, and adding a little more wine if it cooks away, until the duck meat falls away from the bones, about 1½ hours. Discard the bones, thyme, and bay leaf.

Spoon the duck into a small earthenware pot. Pour in any cooking liquid from the saucepan and cool. Cover and refrigerate.

SALADE DE MAGRET FUMÉ

SMOKED DUCK BREAST SALAD

Anyone visiting the markets of southwest France will notice the quantities of duck breeders selling smoked magrets de canard—dark, delicious, smoked breasts of duck sheathed in marbled fat. Bernard Mounet (wholeheartedly acknowledged as the Roi de Canard *throughout the region) gave us this ultrasimple recipe for a duck breast salad when we visited his farm. Serve it with red wine, he advises, and good company.*

Serves 6

3 tablespoons red wine vinegar
1 tablespoon Dijon mustard
⅓ cup plus 1 tablespoon olive oil
1 tablespoon walnut oil
1 curly lettuce, washed
4 ounces watercress, washed
2 smoked duck breasts
Sea salt, to taste
Freshly ground black pepper, to taste
1 cup (4 ounces) walnuts, coarsely chopped
A bunch of chervil, leaves finely chopped

Whisk the vinegar and mustard in a small bowl, and gradually whisk in the olive and walnut oils. Break the lettuce into a large bowl and add the watercress. Slice the duck as thinly as possible across the grain. Add to the greens with the vinaigrette and mix well. Season with salt and pepper. Add the walnuts and chervil and toss again. Serve at once.

CONFIT DE CANARD

DUCK CONFIT

Confit de canard is one of the principal ingredients of cassoulet (page 158), although it makes an irresistible dish on its own. You can buy it from any market in the Southwest region, but nothing beats the homemade version, which can be eaten warm and crispy right after cooking, or aged in the refrigerator for a deeper, more complex flavor. You'll find duck legs and the rendered fat at many specialty butchers and online.

Serves 6

6 duck legs
¼ cup sea salt
Freshly ground black pepper, to taste
6 sprigs of thyme
6 bay leaves
2¼ pounds rendered goose or duck fat

Rub the duck all over with some of the salt and season with the pepper. Place the duck in a deep roasting pan, cover with the salt, and add the thyme and bay leaves. Cover and refrigerate overnight.

Heat the oven to 300°F. Remove the duck from the salt mixture, brush away the salt, and reserve the herbs. Return the duck to the pan and add the fat. Bake until tender, about 2 hours, basting occasionally and turning the duck halfway through cooking. Heat a very large glass canning jar to hold the duck in the oven for 5 minutes. Transfer the duck to the hot jar. Add the reserved herbs. Strain the fat into the jar until the meat is totally covered. Cool, then close the jar. Refrigerate for 1 day or up to 2 months.

To serve, remove the duck from the fat and remove the excess clinging fat. Cook in a very large skillet over medium heat, turning occasionally, until the skin is golden and crisp, about 15 minutes. Remove the thyme and bay leaves. Serve hot.

POULET CHAUSSEUR

HUNTER-STYLE CHICKEN

Wild mushrooms, often gathered from the forest, are responsible for the name of this fragrant dish. This traditional dish relies on the quality of its ingredients. Free-range chickens are the best, locally bred and corn-fed.

Serves 6

3 tablespoons unsalted butter
3 tablespoons olive oil
2 (3-pound) free-range chickens, cut into serving pieces
Sea salt, to taste
Freshly ground black pepper, to taste
10 ounces cremini mushrooms, sliced
3 shallots, chopped
2 garlic cloves, chopped
⅓ cup plus 1 tablespoon all-purpose flour
¾ cup dry white wine
1⅔ cups chicken stock
1 tablespoon tomato paste
A bunch of tarragon, leaves chopped
A bunch of flat-leaf parsley, leaves chopped
A bunch of chervil, leaves chopped

Heat the butter and oil together in a Dutch oven over medium-high heat. Season the chickens with salt and pepper. In batches, brown the chicken, about 7 minutes, and transfer to a platter. Add the mushrooms, shallots, and garlic to the pot and cook over medium heat until the mushrooms soften, about 8 minutes. Sprinkle in the flour and mix well. Gradually stir in the wine and then the stock and tomato paste. Bring to a boil. Return the chicken to the pot, cover, and reduce the heat to medium-low. Cook until the chicken shows no sign of pink when pierced at the bone, about 30 minutes. Stir in the tarragon, parsley, and chervil and serve hot.

PÂTÉ DE FOIE

CHICKEN LIVER PÂTÉ

The southwest of France is well known for the variety and excellence of its terrines and pâtés, although few people realize how simple these can be to make at home. This chicken liver pâté is both quick and delicious to prepare, and can be adapted by adding chestnuts, mushrooms, walnuts, or any other seasonal ingredients to suit any occasion. Serve with hot toast and green salad.

Serves 6

1¼ pounds chicken livers
10 tablespoons (1¼ sticks) unsalted butter
2 shallots, finely chopped
2 garlic cloves, chopped
⅓ cup red wine
3 tablespoons heavy cream
Sea salt, to taste
Freshly ground black pepper, to taste
A large sprig of thyme

Trim the chicken livers and cut into even-sized pieces. Heat 5 tablespoons butter in a large skillet over high heat. In batches, cook the livers until seared on all sides, 4 to 5 minutes. Transfer the livers to a food processor fitted with the chopping blade. Add the shallots and cook over medium-low heat until softened, about 4 minutes. Add the garlic and cook for 2 minutes more. Add the shallot mixture to the livers. Add the red wine to the skillet and bring to a boil. Pour into the food processor, along with the cream, salt, and pepper and process the liver mixture until smooth. Pack the pâté into a serving bowl or ramekin and smooth the top. Melt the remaining 5 tablespoons butter in a small saucepan with the thyme. Remove the thyme, and place it on the pâté, then pour the butter into the bowl to cover the pâté. Cool, cover, and refrigerate for at least 1 hour before serving.

POULET À LA MOUTARDE DE DIJON

CHICKEN BREASTS WITH DIJON MUSTARD

This is a quick, easy-to-make dish that works especially well as a light summer meal. Serve with fresh watercress tossed in vinaigrette.

Serves 6

6 tablespoons Dijon mustard
Zest and juice from 2 unwaxed lemons
2 teaspoons sweet paprika
3 garlic cloves, chopped
6 bone-in chicken breasts
Olive oil, for the baking pan

Mix the mustard, lemon zest and juice, paprika, and garlic in a small bowl. Spread generously over the chicken breasts. Cover and let stand at room temperature for 1 hour.

Heat the oven to 350°F. Lightly oil a baking sheet. Place the chicken breasts and any clinging marinade on the baking sheet. Bake until there is no sign of pink when the breast is pierced in the thickest part with a knife, about 45 minutes.

TERRINE DE CAMPAGNE

COUNTRY-STYLE PORK PÂTÉ

A meat terrine is traditionally made in an earthenware terrine dish, which ensures that it cooks evenly, but you can use a loaf pan instead. Serve it sliced, with crusty bread and a fresh green salad. Pistachios work well in this terrine, giving it a slightly sweet flavor and crunchy texture: add about 4 ounces chopped pistachios to the final mixture and garnish with a few whole nuts on top.

1 pound sliced bacon

8 ounces chicken livers, trimmed

1¼ pounds boneless pork loin roast, trimmed and cut into ½-inch dice

8 ounces ground pork

4 shallots, finely chopped

2 large eggs, beaten

A bunch of flat-leaf parsley, leaves chopped

4 sprigs of thyme, leaves stripped from stems

2 bay leaves, finely chopped

Sea salt, to taste

Freshly ground black pepper, to taste

Heat the oven to 325°F. Chop ¼ pound of the bacon and the chicken livers and place in a large bowl. Add the diced pork, ground pork, shallots, eggs, parsley, thyme, and bay leaves. Season with the salt and pepper, being generous with the salt. Line a 9- by 5-inch terrine dish or loaf pan with most of the remaining bacon strips, saving some for the top. Fill compactly with the meat mixture and smooth the top. Fold over the excess bacon strips, and lay the remaining slices on top. Bake until a meat thermometer inserted in the center reads 165°F, about 1½ hours. Cool for 30 minutes, then carefully pour off the excess meat juices. Place a weight that fits snugly on top of the terrine (such as another loaf pan filled with canned food) and compress it for 1½ hours.

If you prefer an unmolded terrine, invert and unmold it at this point. In either case, cover and refrigerate the terrine overnight before slicing and serving. The terrine can be refrigerated for up to 7 days.

Desserts

The first impact is always visual. The shapes, colors, and designs of the French pâtisserie take the concept of dessert far beyond mere appetite and into performance art. The jeweled cakes are lifted carefully into their presentation boxes, decorated with paper flowers and long curls of multicolored ribbon. This takes time; it demands reverence. There is an unspoken etiquette both in the buying and in the eating of these little pieces of whimsy, a general understanding of the work that has gone into their creation. Still, for me the real delight is the atmosphere of the place: the mingled scents of caramel, of fruits preserved in Armagnac, of chocolate, mocha, vanilla, and freshly baked croissants. And the anticipation of flavors—fresh fruits on *pâte brisée* and *crème anglaise*; bitter chocolate sprinkled over the bright green icing of a *Salammbô;* a fat baba soaking regally in sugar and dark rum . . .

It would be futile to try to duplicate the spectacular work of those master pâtissiers. However, there are plenty more ways to explore and enjoy those luscious ingredients. This section provides a few ideas on how to adapt and re-create at home some of France's best-loved desserts and pastries.

French tradition uses desserts sparingly, but to effect. Most families will usually end a meal with cheese, fruit, or yogurt during the week, but at weekends, the celebratory dessert comes into its own. Every village has its pâtisserie, and on Sunday mornings the shop window will be artfully crammed with cakes, tarts, and *pièces montées*—those elegant mountains of choux buns mortared together with caramel and chocolate.

CRÈME CARAMEL

This silken, unctuous dish belongs to the large family of crèmes renversées—*cream-based dishes baked in a water bath and served upside down—and this version remains one of the best known and best loved of French desserts. Alexandre Dumas suggests a variety of alternative flavors—rosewater, pistachio, lemon, coffee—but in all cases, the basic technique remains the same.*

Serves 6

Caramel
⅔ cup superfine sugar

Custard
2¾ cups milk
4 large eggs
½ cup superfine sugar
1 vanilla bean

For the caramel: Melt the sugar in a heavy-bottomed, small saucepan over low heat. Once the sugar has melted, increase the heat to medium-high and cook until it is a golden caramel brown. Pour the caramel into six ¾-cup ramekins, turning to coat the bottoms completely. Cool.

Heat the oven to 350°F. Heat the milk in a saucepan over low heat to a shivering simmer. Beat the eggs and sugar in a bowl, then add the hot milk and mix well. Cut the vanilla bean in half lengthwise; scrape out the seeds with the tip of a knife into the custard. Pour into the ramekins, stirring the custard after each pour to distribute the vanilla seeds. Place the ramekins in a deep roasting pan and add enough hot water to come 1 inch up the sides of the ramekins. Bake until the custards feel set to the touch, about 35 minutes.

Remove the ramekins from the water and cool completely. (Refrigerate overnight, if you wish.) Press around the edges of each custard to loosen it from the sides of the ramekin. Invert and unmold each custard and its caramel onto individual plates.

BAVAROISE AU CAFÉ

COFFEE BAVARIAN CREAM

There are any number of variants on the classic bavaroise, the most elegant of chilled puddings. I particularly love the chocolate and black currant versions—for these, substitute the coffee in this recipe with either cocoa powder or crème de cassis. If, like me, you prefer not to use gelatin, just refrigerate the bavaroise overnight for a firmer consistency.

Serves 6

1¾ cups milk
3 tablespoons coarsely ground coffee
⅓ cup sugar
4 large egg yolks
4 teaspoons unflavored granulated gelatin
1 cup heavy cream
Whipped cream, for garnish
Bittersweet chocolate (about 2 ounces),
    for garnish

Heat 1½ cups milk in a medium saucepan until almost boiling. Stir in the coffee and let stand for 5 minutes. Whisk the sugar and yolks in a medium bowl until very light and fluffy. Strain the hot milk through a fine sieve to remove the coffee, then beat the milk into the yolks. Return to the saucepan and cook over low heat, stirring constantly with a wooden spoon, until the mixture is thick enough to coat the spoon—do not let come near a boil! Meanwhile, sprinkle the gelatin over the remaining ¼ cup milk in a small bowl and let stand 5 minutes to soften. Add to the hot custard and stir well to dissolve the gelatin. Pour into a bowl, press plastic wrap directly on the surface, and cool.

Beat the cream until soft peaks form, then fold into the cooled coffee mixture. Pour into 6 individual glasses. Cover each with plastic wrap and refrigerate a few hours until chilled. Garnish each with whipped cream and chocolate curls (use a potato peeler). Serve chilled.

SEMOULE AU CITRON

POLENTA AND LEMON CAKE

*This Moorish dish may have come to France as far
back as the Crusades. Combining cornmeal for its
rich, dense texture and lemon for its sharp, sweet
taste, it is excellent served on its own or with
vanilla ice cream or a simple sauce of red
summer fruits.*

Serves 4 to 6

8 tablespoons (1 stick) unsalted butter,
   plus more for the dish
¼ cup milk
1 vanilla bean, split lengthwise
⅓ cup plus 1 tablespoon yellow cornmeal
⅓ cup plus 1 tablespoon self-rising flour
½ cup confectioners' sugar
3 large eggs
2 tablespoons Armagnac
Zest and juice of 1 unwaxed lemon

Heat the oven to 350°F. Butter an 8-inch-
round baking dish. Heat the 8 tablespoons
butter and the milk in a saucepan until hot.
Scrape the vanilla seeds into the milk. Mix
the cornmeal, flour, and confectioners' sugar
in a medium bowl, and make a well in the
center.

   Whisk the eggs in a medium bowl, and
gradually whisk in the hot milk. Pour into the
well and mix until smooth. Stir in the
Armagnac and lemon zest and juice. Spread in
the baking dish. Bake until golden and the
cakes spring back when pressed in the center,
about 25 minutes. Cool, and cut into wedges
to serve. Serve warm or cold.

BRIOCHE PERDU

A number of French recipes are designed to use stale bread. This elegant version of bread-and-butter pudding (also known as French toast) works very well with fresh or stale brioche—but to be honest, does anyone ever let brioche go stale?—and the addition of floc (see page 60) gives a grown-up sophistication to a comfort-food favorite.

Serves 6

6 tablespoons (¾ stick) unsalted butter,
    softened
6 thick slices brioche loaf, about 10
    ounces total
3 or 4 cooking apples, such as Golden
    Delicious, peeled, cored, and sliced
¾ cup raisins
1¼ cups milk
3 large eggs
⅓ cup white floc or semidry white wine
¼ cup packed dark brown sugar,
    preferably Demerara

Butter a baking dish to hold the brioche and spread the slices with butter. Scatter the apples and raisins on the bottom of the dish. Arrange the brioche slices in overlapping layers on top of the fruit. Whisk the milk, eggs, and floc in a bowl and pour over the brioche, being sure to coat all the slices. Using a spatula, push the brioche down to enable the egg mix to be soaked into the brioche. Scatter the brown sugar over the top. Refrigerate for at least 1 hour or overnight.

    Heat the oven to 300°F. Bake until the custard has set and the top is golden brown, about 45 minutes. Serve hot.

PÊCHES AU CARDINAL

PEACHES IN RED RASPBERRY SAUCE

Quite a number of classic French desserts seem to come to us via members of the clergy. I'm not sure who the original cardinal was (although I like to think it was Cardinal Richelieu, the arch-enemy of Dumas' The Three Musketeers*), but this has got to be one of the most delicious ways of serving fresh peaches. Fran advises blending and sieving the raspberries, while I prefer the sauce to be more as nature intended. If you're feeling truly irredeemable, substitute a tablespoon of raspberry or black currant liqueur in place of the water.*

Serves 6

6 ripe peaches
12 ounces fresh raspberries
7 ounces (1¾ cups) confectioners' sugar
½ cup sliced almonds, toasted

Plunge the peaches in a pot of boiling water for 40 seconds. Drain, cool for a few minutes, then peel off the skin with a paring knife. Cut each peach in half and remove the pit. Place each in its own serving bowl, cover, and refrigerate to chill. Puree the raspberries and confectioners' sugar and 1 tablespoon water in a blender. Rub through a fine wire sieve to remove the seeds. Pour the raspberry sauce over the peaches, sprinkle with the almonds, and serve chilled.

PETITS POTS AU CITRON

BERRIES WITH LEMON CREAM

These colorful little lemon-berry pots are the ideal light dessert for summer, combining fresh seasonal berries with tangy lemon cream. Lovely with ladyfinger cookies and crème fraîche. If you wish, use other soft fruit in season, such as apricots or peaches. Simply halve, pit, and chop the fruit before putting it in the ramekins.

Serves 6

1 pint blueberries
4 large eggs
⅔ cup superfine sugar
Zest and juice of 3 unwaxed lemons
1 cup plus 2 tablespoons heavy cream
⅔ cup confectioners' sugar, for topping

Heat the oven to 300°F. Divide the berries among six 8-ounce ramekins.

Whisk the eggs, superfine sugar, and lemon zest and juice in a medium bowl until smooth. Stir in the cream. Pour equal amounts of the lemon cream into the ramekins. Place the lemon pots into a large roasting pan. Add enough hot water to come halfway up the sides of the ramekins. Carefully place the pan in the oven. Bake until the lemon cream looks set, about 30 minutes. Remove the ramekins from the water and cool completely. Refrigerate, if you wish.

When ready to serve, preheat the broiler on high. Sift a generous amount of confectioners' sugar over each ramekin. Broil until the sugar melts and turns a golden caramel color. Cool again before serving.

TARTE AUX CERISES

CHERRY TARTS

I think the cherry makes for the most beautiful of fresh fruit tarts, although, of course, you can use whatever fruit appeals to you according to the season. For me, though, the cherry is the perfect fruit, and there are so many different species to choose from at various times of the year in France: the fat black Morello cherry, the bright red cherries of early summer, the musky-flavored yellow ones of autumn, or the sour-sweet griottes that are exceptional soaked in brandy.

Serves 6

Sweet Pastry Dough
1¾ cups all-purpose flour
10 tablespoons (1¼ sticks) unsalted butter, chilled, cut into small cubes, plus more for buttering the pans
¾ cup confectioners' sugar, plus more for rolling out the dough
2 large egg yolks, beaten

2 tablespoons red currant jelly, melted
¾ cup heavy cream
¾ cup crème fraîche
2 tablespoons kirsch
1 pound fresh cherries, pitted (reserve a few with stems for garnish)
1 tablespoon confectioners' sugar, for garnish

For the *pâté sablée:* Sift the flour into a large bowl. Add the butter and rub with your fingertips until the mixture resembles bread crumbs. Stir in the confectioners' sugar. Add the yolks and mix well with a round-bladed knife in a cutting motion until the pastry comes together. Flatten into a disk, wrap in plastic wrap, and refrigerate for 30 minutes. Lightly butter 6 individual tart pans. Dust a cool work surface with confectioners' sugar. Roll out the dough ⅛ inch thick. Line the pans, and refrigerate for 30 minutes.

Heat the oven to 350°F. Line each pan with aluminum foil and dried beans. Bake for 10 minutes. Carefully remove the foil and beans and bake until the shells are golden, about 15 minutes. Cool.

Brush the bottoms of the pastry shells with the jelly. Whip the cream just until it holds soft peaks, and whisk in the crème fraîche and kirsch. Spread the cream filling in each tart. Top with the pitted cherries and garnish with the cherries with stems. Sift with confectioners' sugar and serve.

ÎLES FLOTTANTES

FLOATING ISLANDS

These "floating islands" have been popular for hundreds of years, and make a spectacular, and only slightly fiddly, dessert to prepare.

Serves 6

Custard
2¼ cups milk
½ cup sugar, preferably turbinado
1 vanilla bean, split lengthwise
5 large eggs yolks

Meringues
3 large egg whites, at room temperature
⅓ cup plus 2 tablespoons superfine sugar

Toasted sliced almonds, for garnish
½ cup sugar, preferably turbinado, for
   caramel

For the custard: Heat the milk and sugar in a medium saucepan over low heat. Scrape the vanilla seeds from the bean into the milk. Whisk the yolks in a heatproof medium bowl, and whisk in the hot milk. Fill a skillet with 1 inch of water and bring to a simmer over medium heat. Place the bowl in the skillet and whisk until it thickens into a light-bodied custard, about 10 minutes. Pour it into 6 individual bowls. Cover the custard with plastic wrap pressed directly on the surface and cool.

For the meringues: Line a baking sheet with a clean kitchen towel. Half-fill a large, wide skillet with water and bring to a gentle simmer. Beat the egg whites with an electric mixer on high speed until soft peaks form. Gradually whisk in the sugar to make shiny, stiff peaks. Using 2 dessertspoons, shape 3 or 4 egg-shaped meringues and gently place them as they are shaped into the water. Simmer for 30 seconds, then turn and cook until they hold their shape, about 30 seconds more. Use a slotted spoon to transfer them to the kitchen towel to remove excess water. Repeat with the remaining meringue to make 12 islands.

Uncover the custard. Place 2 meringues in each bowl and sprinkle with the almonds. Cook the sugar in a small saucepan over medium-high heat until it melts and turns into a golden caramel. Drizzle the caramel over the tops of the meringues. Traditionally, this dish is served chilled, but it is also rather delicious warm.

TARTE BELLE HÉLÈNE

PEAR AND CHOCOLATE TART

Pears and chocolate have always been something of a winning combination. Use firm, ripe Bartlett pears for this recipe, and serve just warm with vanilla ice cream and curls of bittersweet chocolate. The pastry is a crumbly sweet one, used only for desserts.

Serves 6

Sweet Pastry Dough
1 cup all-purpose flour
5 tablespoons unsalted butter, chilled, cut into small cubes, plus more for the pan
⅓ cup confectioners' sugar, plus more for rolling out the dough
2 large egg yolks, beaten

Filling
3 ripe Bartlett pears, peeled, halved lengthwise, and cored
6 tablespoons unsalted butter, at room temperature
⅓ cup sugar
1 large egg
2 tablespoons ground almonds (grind sliced almonds in a blender)
⅔ cup self-rising flour

¼ cup cocoa powder
¼ teaspoon baking powder
3 tablespoons milk

Heat the oven to 375°F. Lightly butter a 9-inch springform pan.

For the pastry: Sift the flour into a medium bowl. Add the butter and rub with your fingertips until the mixture resembles bread crumbs. Stir in the confectioners' sugar. Mixing with a round-bladed knife in a cutting motion, add enough of the yolks to bring the pastry together. Flatten into a disk, wrap in plastic wrap, and refrigerate for 30 minutes. Lightly butter 6 individual tart pans. Dust a cool work surface with confectioners' sugar. Roll out the dough into a 9-inch round. Carefully roll the dough over the rolling pin and unroll it into the pan. Press the dough gently into the pan bottom, and refrigerate for 30 minutes.

For the filling: Arrange the pear halves round side up in the pan. Beat the butter and sugar until light and fluffy. Beat in the egg, then the almonds. Sift the flour, cocoa, and baking powder into the butter mixture. Add the milk and fold until the batter is smooth. Pour into the pan and smooth the top. Bake for 30 minutes. Tent the pan with aluminum foil and bake until the filling feels set when pressed in the center, about 15 minutes more. Cool.

COMPOTE DE POMMES AUX PRUNEAUX D'AGEN

APPLES AND AGEN PRUNES COMPOTE

Most French families have a version of this recipe, which makes the most of any fruit in season. In this recipe, the prunes and spices give an almost mulled taste to the autumn apples, which can be eaten on their own or chilled and topped with whipped cream and chocolate curls for a more festive look.

Serves 6

1 pound Agen prunes or moist California
    dried plums
8 apples, peeled, cored, and cut into
    wedges
¾ cup packed dark brown sugar, preferably
    muscavado
2 teaspoons apple pie spice

Heat the oven to 350°F. Mix the prunes and apples in a baking dish. Sprinkle with the brown sugar and apple pie spice, then stir in 1½ cups water. Cover and bake until the apples are tender, about 1 hour. Cool. The compote gets better and richer with time, so if possible, make it at least a day ahead and store in the refrigerator.

CROISSANTS

Croissants are the essential French pastry. Fresh baked for breakfast or smothered in almonds for the goûter *(snacktime), there's something wonderful about the flaky, almost brittle crust and the soft, fragrant center of these simple little pastries. Of course, you can buy croissants (or what purport to be croissants) from supermarkets everywhere, but believe me, nothing beats the real deal, baked to perfection in your own oven and eaten warm, with a cup of bitter hot chocolate. To have croissants ready to bake in the morning, refrigerate the shaped triangles overnight.*

Makes 12 to 14 croissants

3½ cups unbleached flour
3 tablespoons sugar
1 teaspoon salt
¾ cup lukewarm water
⅓ cup plus 1 tablespoon lukewarm milk
2 (¼-ounce) packages active dry yeast
10 tablespoons (1¼ sticks) unsalted
   butter, at cool room temperature, plus
   more for the baking sheet
1 large egg, beaten, for glazing

Sift the flour, sugar, and salt into a large bowl. Combine the warm water and milk in a small bowl and sprinkle in the yeast. Let stand 5 minutes, then stir to dissolve. Make a well in the center of the flour and pour in the dissolved yeast. Stir to make a stiff dough. Shape into a ball, cover with plastic wrap, and refrigerate for 30 minutes.

Place the butter between 2 sheets of waxed paper. Beat and roll it with a rolling pin to make a flat 7-inch square. Lightly flour a work surface and roll out the dough into a 14-inch square. Place the butter in the center with 2 points facing north and south. Fold the dough over to cover the butter and pinch the seams closed. Add more flour to the work surface and dust the top of the dough with flour. Roll out the dough into a rectangle about 9 by 18 inches. Dust off any excess flour, and fold the dough like a letter, one-third down, and the other up. Turn 90 degrees, and roll and fold again as described. Wrap in plastic wrap and refrigerate for 30 minutes. Repeat the double rolling, folding, and resting two more times.

Cut an 8- by 8- by 5-inch triangle from cardboard for a template. Lightly butter a large baking sheet.

Roll out the dough into a 16-inch square. Cut the dough in half horizontally. Using the template, cut out triangles of dough. Starting at the base, roll up each triangle, shape into a crescent, and place on the baking sheet with the point underneath so the croissants do not unravel. Cover with plastic wrap and let stand in a warm, draft-free place until doubled in volume, about 1 hour. (Or refrigerate overnight.)

Heat the oven to 225°F. Brush each croissant lightly with the beaten egg. Bake until golden brown, about 15 minutes. Serve warm.

Almond Croissants: When the croissants are baked, split each in half horizontally with a serrated knife and spread with softened almond paste. Sandwich together, and spread the top with a little more almond paste, sprinkle with toasted almonds, and sift with confectioners' sugar. To make your own almond paste, process 1 cup sliced almonds, ¾ cup superfine sugar, and 2 tablespoons unsalted butter in a food processor.

CHICHIS

SOUTHWEST BEIGNETS

These frivolous little sugared pastries are available fresh at most markets throughout southwestern France, and the smell of their cooking is intoxicating. Eat them hot and dusted with confectioners' sugar or with a generous spoonful of fruit preserves.

Serves 4 to 6

1 (¼-ounce) package active dry yeast
3 tablespoons sugar, preferably turbinado
¾ cup warm (105° to 115°F) milk
2 cups all-purpose flour
2 large egg yolks, beaten
Vegetable oil, for deep-frying
Superfine sugar, for garnish

Dissolve the yeast and sugar in the milk. Sift the flour into a medium bowl and make a well in the center. Mix the yolks with the yeast mixture and pour into the flour. Stir to make a smooth soft dough, then knead on a floured surface for 10 minutes. Place the bowl in a lightly oiled bowl. Cover with plastic wrap and let stand in a warm place until doubled, about 1 hour. Knead lightly on the floured work surface. Roll portions of the dough into 2-inch-long sausages. Cover and let stand for 10 minutes.

Heat 2 to 3 inches of oil in a large deep saucepan over high heat to 350°F. A few at a time, add the dough sausages and fry until golden all over (they will sink and resurface). Using a slotted spoon, transfer to paper towels to drain, and roll generously in the superfine sugar.

GÂTEAU BASQUE

BASQUE CAKE

This delicious, moist cake originates from the Basque region, where almonds are plentiful and used in many types of pastry.

Serves 6

Filling
1⅔ cups milk
1 vanilla bean, split in half lengthwise
5 large egg yolks
1 cup sugar, preferably turbinado
¼ cup ground almonds
3 tablespoon all-purpose flour

Almond Pastry Dough
2½ cups all-purpose flour
8 tablespoons (1 stick) unsalted butter, at
    room temperature, plus extra for the pan
1 cup confectioners' sugar, plus extra for
    rolling out the dough
½ cup ground almonds (grind sliced
    almonds in a blender)
Zest of 1 unwaxed lemon
3 to 4 large egg yolks, beaten
½ cup raspberry or red currant preserves
1 large egg yolk, beaten, for brushing
Confectioners' sugar, for garnish

For the filling: Heat the milk in a heavy-bottomed medium saucepan over medium heat. Scrape in the vanilla seeds. Whisk the yolks and sugar in a medium bowl, then mix in the almonds and flour. Slowly whisk in the hot milk. Return the mixture to the saucepan and cook over low heat, stirring constantly, just until it comes to a boil. Transfer to a bowl, cover with plastic wrap pressed on the surface, and cool completely.

For the almond pastry dough: Sift the flour into a large bowl, add the butter, and rub with your fingertips until the mixture resembles bread crumbs. Stir in the confectioners' sugar, almonds, and lemon zest. Using a round-bladed knife, stir in enough of the yolks until the dough comes together. Shape into a disk, wrap in plastic wrap, and refrigerate for 30 minutes. Lightly butter a 9-inch-round springform pan. Dust a cool work surface with confectioners' sugar. Roll three-quarters of the dough into a 12-inch round. Carefully roll the dough over the rolling pin and unroll it into the pan. Press the dough gently into the pan bottom, and refrigerate for 30 minutes. Roll out the remaining dough into a 9-inch round and refrigerate separately.

Heat the oven to 350°F. Spread the jam over the bottom of the dough in the pan, then spread with the filling. Brush the edges of the dough with the egg and place the lid on top. Trim the edges and crimp together. Score the top of the pastry with a knife in a crisscross pattern and brush with egg. Bake until golden brown, tenting the cake with aluminum foil if it seems to be browning too much, about 45 minutes. Cool at least 30 minutes, and sift with confectioners' sugar before serving.

PAIN AUX NOIX

WALNUT LOAF

This sweet walnut loaf is the perfect accompaniment to cheese and fruit. The loaf is best when made a day in advance.

Makes one 9-inch loaf

14 tablespoons (1¾ sticks) unsalted
  butter, plus more for the pan
1¾ cups coarsely chopped walnuts
½ cup packed light brown sugar
⅓ cup honey
1¼ cups milk
2 large eggs, beaten
2⅔ cups self-rising flour
1 teaspoon baking powder
Confectioners' sugar, for garnish

Heat the oven to 350°F. Butter a 9- by 5-inch loaf pan, and line the bottom and sides with parchment paper. Process the walnuts in a food processor until finely ground.

Melt the butter, sugar, and honey in a medium saucepan over low heat. Remove from the heat and stir in the walnuts. Whisk the milk and eggs together, stir into the pan, then add the flour and baking powder and stir until smooth. Spread in the pan. Bake for 30 minutes. Reduce the heat to 300°F and bake until the cake springs back when pressed, about 30 minutes more. Cool 10 minutes, remove from the pan, and cool completely. Wrap in aluminum foil and age for 1 day. Sift the confectioners' sugar on top before serving.

Special Dedication

In 2003, I decided to donate my part of the proceeds from *The French Kitchen* to Médecins Sans Frontières, an organization I have supported for many years which provides essential medical aid for some of the poorest and most troubled countries in the world.

That year I went with MSF to the Congo to see for myself how the money was being used to combat sleeping sickness, a fatal disease if left untreated, which kills up to half a million people a year. We traveled up the Congo by canoe and riverboat, screening and treating whole villages for the disease. Without treatment, every person who tested positive would have died.

In a society where the idea of miracles has become irrelevant and outdated, it's hard to imagine the true impact of this. In a society where it is considered almost normal for African children to die of easily curable diseases, it is hard to imagine that one small cookbook—or even two—can make much of a difference.

Believe me, it can.

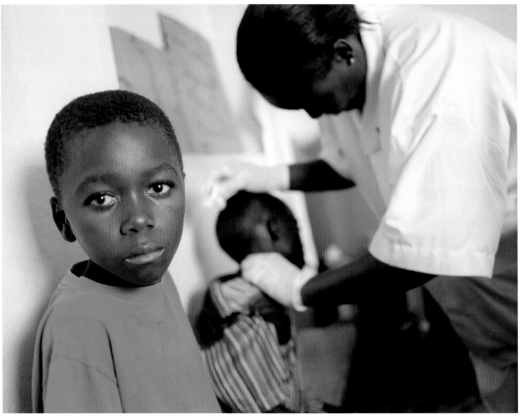

Photo by Tom Craig

This is Boniface. He is eight years old, and he owes you his life.

All Joanne Harris's proceeds from The French Market *will go to MSF in order to help them continue their work in the Congo.*

Index

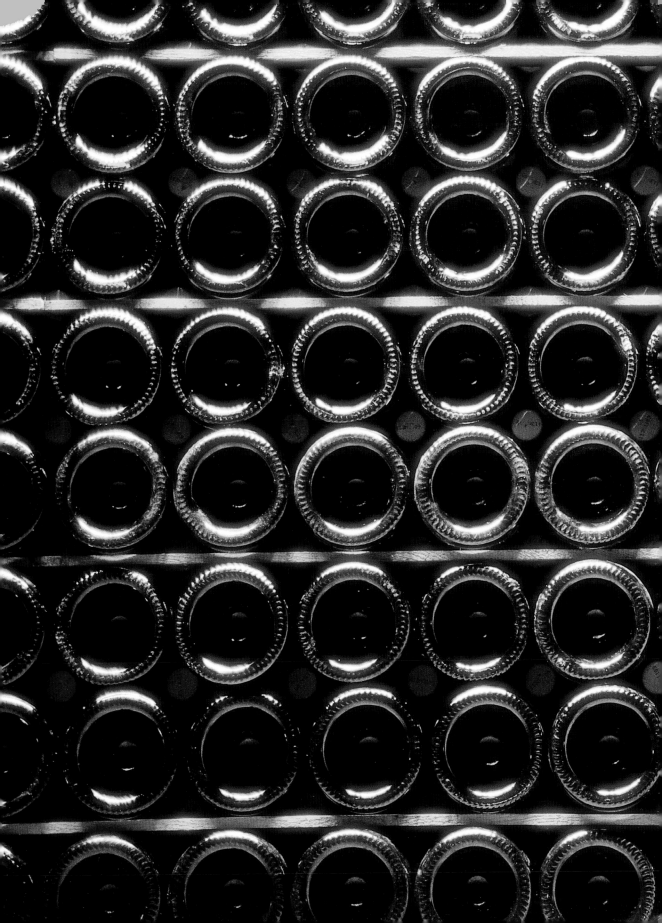

ACKNOWLEDGMENTS

Heartfelt thanks to everyone who helped in the production of this book, especially to:

Madame Labadie, for sharing her family recipes

M. and Mme Sarrauste at the chocolaterie La Cigale

M. Mounet, the Roi du Canard

M. Tadieu, for his award-winning floc

The Baron family, who showed us the largest and tastiest radishes we have ever eaten

Terrance and Angela Stokes, for letting us photograph their wonderful home

Sue and Mike, for their lovely gîte and wealth of local information

Anne-Laure at Laurent Perrier

Caroline at Moët & Chandon

Mark Housden, for lovely props from The French House

Eurostar for a speedy journey to Paris: www.eurostar.co.uk

Serafina Clarke

Stephanie Cabot

Francesca Liversidge

Debi Treloar

Mari Roberts

Fiona Andreanelli

Stuart Haygarth

Helen Trent

Anna Burgess-Lumsden, for assisting in the kitchen

Finally, to all the stallholders at markets in France who so kindly welcomed us, and the local shops back in England who worked hard to find produce to match for photography: Andreas Georghiou fine fruit and vegetables, Mortimer and Bennet deli, Covent Garden fishmongers, Macken Brothers butchers and Fishworks—all on Turnham Green Terrace, London W4.

Thank you to all of you. We could never have done it alone.